The Bosphoru

By Naci V Natji

They won't go when I go
No more lying friends
Wanting tragic ends
Though they do pretend
They won't go when I go

All those bleeding hearts
With sorrows to impart
Were right here from the start
And they won't go when I go

And I'll go where I've longed
To go so long
Away from tears

Gone from painful cries
Away from saddened eyes
Along with him, I'll bide
Because they won't go when I go

Big men feeling small
Weak ones standing tall
I will watch them fall
They won't go when I go

And I'll go where I've longed
To go so long
Away from tears

Unclean minds mislead the pure
The innocent will leave for sure

For them, there is a resting place
People sinning just for fun
They will never see the sun
For they can never show their faces
There ain't no room for the hopeless sinner
Who will take more than he will give
He ain't hardly gonna give

The greed of man will be
Far away from me
And my soul will be free
They won't go when I go

Since my soul conceived
All that I believe
The kingdom I will see
'Cause they won't go when I go

When I go
Where I'll go
No one can keep me
From my destiny

SARAH

"Sabiha Gokcen Airport, Istanbul, Sir?" I nodded my head, trying hard to avoid any eye contact; after all, I was not flying out of England for a holiday. Only I knew why I was going. I had made my mind up and now really wanted to go. I did not have any doubts. It was time. I just focused my sights on the brightly coloured orange badge, pinned slightly above her left breast, announcing to the world in indented cerise-red that her name was Sarah. Out of all the names in this world, she had to be a Sarah. I looked up, and yes, she had blue eyes and yes, she was a blonde, well, more golden-blonde. She looked at me with her trained smile. I returned the gesture for the sake of it as she asked me about any luggage. "No luggage to hand in sir?" I thought to myself I'd better answer her as she did not deserve my insolence. I told her that I had none and was travelling light, as I worked in Turkey and had no need to take anything with me. I looked into her perfectly sunflower-seed shaped eyes and smiled again lazily, what did she know? It was not her fault that another Sarah was one of my past crushes, who also had the same blue eyes. I was travelling light and Turkey was going to be my last stop before I completed my last mission. Living my life, it seemed to me that whatever I needed to do, what may have come naturally to anyone else, felt like a never ending mission to me.

It was bye-bye to England, two disastrous marriages and a failed father figure. I had squandered millions of pounds and was leaving all those broken hearts behind. It was over now, it was finished! Fifty years old and it was time. Death seemed more inviting than life.

I was down and disturbed and wanted to take away all the pain I felt inside. Death would be a better choice.

3

Sarah handed me my boarding pass, she smiled and I acknowledged her courteously and made my way towards the departure lounge. Only I knew how really screwed up I was emotionally. Most people around me thought it was all an act that I behaved the way I did.

I was either trying to pull a scam, or was spoilt, lazy or just wanted the sympathy tag.

For as long as I can remember I had an addiction to food, gambling and self-destructive behavior in my life. Self-harming has always been with me, one way or the other but it is tough to spot addiction unless you experience it.

The last eighteen months had been hell but now I was on my way. No more gambling with my future, no worrying about the risk, no more bosses. I did not care anymore, what could I lose? I felt that I had already lost everything. What a cliché I was - the 'walking dead'. I was the true gambler, an addict. I knew what losing felt like and was by now immune. Ironically whilst walking towards the departure lounge my eyes were attracted to the flashing lights of the games arcade in the terminal. I stopped walking for a few seconds, looked at the fruit machines that had taken hours and hours of my life, stolen thousands of pounds, and exhausted me of many thoughts, sedating my pain, giving back only escapism. This moment reminded me of the quote that I had read sitting on the seat of a betting shop toilet, punching my head, after once again losing all the money I had. "You do anything long enough to escape the habit of living until the escape becomes the habit" - whoever wrote that, sure knew about compulsion. I was addicted to the pain of losing. Losing had become another way of me self-harming. Familiar in defeat, I was contained, I had lost any vision, and I was drifting and crushed. Addiction, or should I say, addictions, had destroyed me. My gambling was now physically under control, forcefully so, because I could no longer afford it. So I had to stop. My addiction of thinking about food, eating, consuming, devouring, and all the cravings was another question. The obsession to eating was, however, one that was impossible to stop. With any other addictions like, say alcoholism, you can stop. The body, mind and soul can willfully be trained to stop taking drugs, drinking alcohol, or stop gambling, because the body is not dependent on them. With food one has to eat to live, or in my case, live to eat. I had to satisfy the emptiness inside, as well as live with and support this mass that I had created since birth.

I had spent the last fifteen years being in a compulsive, neurotic relationship with H. This was the definitive and absolute gamble of my whole life so far. This relationship was as if I had been playing the lottery every second, minute and hour of the day. I had to be in every draw, every spin, knowing that to find happiness with her was a long shot but I consistently bought a ticket, hoping and praying that this was the bet that would win me my jackpot. This Love that I was gambling on, was gambled not with money but with my heart. I always had a chance to win my money back, but might not get my heart back. The last thing you want is to get addicted to someone.

I could smell the departure lounge approaching long before I saw it, the scents from the perfumery, The Chanel's, Prada's and Estee Lauders coming from the duty free shops. Reflecting back, H loved the smell of Chanel Chance perfume. Freshly ground coffee, the lattes, and mochas. The aromas arousing your taste buds floating in the air, the many different kinds of teas being brewed, stirred, and drunk. This time there was nobody, no one to buy for. Usually I would have bought early, before I flew out in case I could not find H's favourites on my way back. Everywhere I looked reminded me of what I had experienced before, all of it was like a dream yet all now gone, just distant memories. Many years had passed, many of me giving all that I had trying to find or even buy some love.

I looked out for the information screens for news on which departure gate I was flying out from and walked on towards that direction. I had a created a habit that I always tried to get on the plane first, and waited last for all the passengers to embark after landing. I would try and avoid any embarrassing moments that I thought or imagined could happen to a very fat man, such as being too wide to walk down the aisle of the plane. The fewer eyes that were looking at me, made me subconsciously feel better, I was not taking any chances, even though this was speedy boarding. Sitting in the departure lounge I thought that I should feel sad and scared. But I didn't.

"Hello sir, plenty of seats at the rear of the plane!" The stewardess smiled at me looking at my boarding pass. She pointed at these seats that always looked smaller than they were but this was my paranoia taking over again. Always worrying if the seats would be wide enough to take my enormous bulk, I sat down, by a window seat as I knew I would not be moving anywhere for the next four or so hours. I could not go through the embarrassment of asking someone to give me way, to go to the toilet. I looked around me and started to ask myself - how did it all come to this? Was this all written? Was this my destiny? How did it all start? How did I get myself into this position? I got comfortable and decided to spend the last of the English money I had in my wallet, I did not need it any more. I asked the steward for a double brandy. I asked for it to be served with a single cube of ice. The ice in the glass was transparent. I knew that you were not supposed to have ice with brandy and that this was not conventional, but I

6

did not do the conventional. The brandy was served in a very flimsy plastic glass.

I turned and looked through the airplane window. The sky was clear for miles, only broken by the sight of the slightly rusted wing of the plane, blue sky and just white clouds. After my second double cognac, it started to work on me, I became relaxed and softly tranquil. I felt that the plane was all mine and I was alone, I felt somewhat holy, just me and some white clouds that looked spiritual and alive. I was seeing imaginary figures walking on the clouds; I remember seeing a penguin, which had no significance in my life. I was not drunk, because I could make the figures disappear and turn them back into clouds again. When the images all became clouds I started to think once again and kept asking myself; did this life have a chance?

The Beginning

My mother and father came to the 'Londra' the capital of England at similar times but both in different circumstances by alternative means. However, they both came here for the same reasons from Cyprus. My mother was from a small village called Lefkara which is on the southern side of the island. She was one of nine siblings and second oldest of five girls. Her elder brother was married and had already had come and settled in London. She was supposed to be seventeen years old but was really only fifteen. Her father got her a fake birth certificate so she could travel independently. She came to England to get rich, so as to help her family and make her life better - the so called Cypriot dream.

When she arrived she had endured the ordeal of travelling for weeks by sea and eventually made her way to London and had no choice but to move into her oldest brother's home. Who, as I recall from what my mother said, did not make my mother's stay a welcoming one. Mother was too nice a person to have complained; even now she is very withdrawn, suppresses her opinion and rarely talks or expresses any bitterness about her eldest brother. Although at times she seemed naive and lacked confidence, she was by no means unwise. I am sure her limited English language skills and familiarization of a completely new culture played an important part. If anything, compared with my father she was the thinker of the two (maybe not the leader in my father's eyes) but she was a very good tactician and diplomat.

My mother was a self -taught dressmaker and knew the basics about operating a sewing machine. She worked for up to eighteen hours a day, putting dresses together from specially cut material in a factory owned by an old Jewish lady just known as 'Mrs. Kay' in the East End of London. My uncle, her brother, would take most of her wages as rent and keep and mother was also obliged to send a proportion of the remaining money to her father to pay back money borrowed to finance her travel to the UK. This money was sent via friends and other relatives who would be going back to Cyprus. If any was left she would save money in a Post Office savings account. Often she would starve herself to save some of the money that she had worked hard for. Knowing my mother though, I doubt she could save much as she was always a generous giver and I'm sure she would have helped anyone who needed it.

Mother was very hard working and likeable, generous in everything she gave, spiritually and physically. My mother was an angel, in that she would give everything to help anyone, to her last penny, then go without. I remember people who knew her saying to me, "If there is a heaven, your mother would be guaranteed a place there." Up to this day, my mother has never fully learnt to speak English, maybe because my dad was always there to take care of things for her. Mother often told me stories of her days when she came to England, the bad times that she had to endure, but one of her stories that is set in my mind because she often repeated it and one that I find hard to forget, is that she often felt cold at night when she tried to sleep. Her brother sold her a very damp ridden, well-used child size quilt that used to belong to her younger nephew. This quilt always had a urine smell embedded into it that would never go, however many times she had washed it. Whenever the temperature dropped and she tried to snuggle into it she could feel the damp that it had absorbed through the day and could smell her brother's son's accidents whilst he was a child. My mother would often tell me the story, whenever she remembered it, emphasizing how her brother had sold this second hand, soiled bed covering to her for an extortionate price and the only way she could afford it was to pay him weekly.

My father came to London about the same time. I don't know who came first. He grew up in Limassol which was a main city in Cyprus. He lived in the Greek side and spoke fluent Greek. He also wanted to follow the Cypriot dream. Dad in a way, was more fortunate than my mother as he had help to finance his journey to 'Londra', or should I say voyage: he had convinced a captain of a cargo ship to allow him to travel on board his vessel, proving to the captain that he was fluent in English, Greek and of course Turkish. This knowledge would help if he was needed to translate. Dad came to the UK via Morocco and touched on Egypt before touring Europe. I do not know how many times he had told me of his adventures.

Whenever the film Casablanca was repeatedly showing on television, he would go into some story on what happened in Morocco whilst travelling to the UK. He would also tell me how he survived on the money that was given to him by one of the many English girlfriends he became acquainted with whilst mingling with the British soldiers based in Limassol. Dad learnt to speak English very quickly in Cyprus from his associations with the British Army. This knowledge also helped him when he arrived in London's Bethnal Green area and although alone, found it easier when settling in his new environment.

His girlfriend in Cyprus apparently was a Scottish army officer's wife. I knew her as Eileen, she not only helped him with the money that she gave him but more importantly, provided him with contact details where he could live once he had arrived in London. With Eileen's help, he was introduced to his landlady who was a widow of another army officer.

Father was a good looking young man, who spoke English with a Mediterranean accent; his olive skin and the sparkle he possessed in his eyes could charm anyone. People for years afterwards used to compare him to Elvis Presley. I am sure he did not only rent a room from the landlady. I constantly heard how she was very obliging in helping him settle in London.

Dad was also was a very good dancer, using his own words, "I could do a good Elvis, better than the King himself, I could teach Bill Haley to rock around the clock!" Once in London he did not have any difficulty making girlfriends. These women helped him in his education on how to survive, where everything was locally as well as on how to spend his money. What he did not spend in the dance halls, he would have spent in the local betting shops.

Dad had been an apprentice carpenter from the age of eight years old, so was at an advantage when he came to London. He knew no one but soon found work – his landlady showed him where to look. Hackney in East London is a well-known 'chippy area' (carpentry and timber) and my father soon found a job in a workshop making beer crates for the Romford brewery. He soon met and became friends with a Turkish Cypriot man who was the general cleaner in the workshop. He later learnt that he was the grandfather of my mother's sister in law. The old man took a shine to my Dad, telling him that he 'needed' looking after and that he knew the ideal person, my Mother!

My mum and dad were not related and had never heard of each other, him being from the city and my mother from a small rural village. They were introduced and without any fuss were quickly engaged. My father impatiently pressured my mother's family for the two of them to marry quickly. My

11

mother was not happy living with her brother, and my dad needed looking after. There was no reason for the two needy souls not to become one and they soon got married in Shoreditch Town Register office.

Their first home was in an attic room in a house shared by many others. They both worked hard to make a life together. My father was eight years older than my mother, more experienced, a 'Jack the lad 'character, whilst my mother was this innocent, a young women who became totally dependent on my father. She soon became pregnant. I was born in November 1962 at Hackney Hospital. It was a lot easier in the early 1960's to be housed in London and we were very quickly given a council home. The three of us soon moved into a ground floor flat in The Guinness Trust Buildings in Bethnal Green. The home was made up of a single bedroom, a small lounge and a kitchen, which was a palace for us. The building had communal shared toilets and a bathroom on each floor. These were shared by three other families. This arrangement was very hard on my mother because of her very limited understanding of English.

My father had always told me of the difficulties that they both had endured. A lot of it discriminatory, he often repeated the racist comments my mother and he were subjected to. Both of them dreaded having a bath or using the toilet. Often he would come out of the bathroom and be confronted with a racist remark or comments such as "Is it that time of the month again?" and "Why are you washing yourself, you can't wash that 'colour' away?" And told how lucky they were to benefit from running water! My dad understood but kept quiet, ignoring all the neighbourly remarks even as they were embedded in him and in my opinion, hurt him, but he would not have admitted it. My mother's experiences were more of intimidation. Soon my mum would not use the bathroom without my dad accompanying her. My dad would look out and wait outside whilst my mother quickly washed, for fear that someone would be in the corridor, to avoid being taunted. Both my parents were humbled and grateful for being able to live in England. They definitely did not want trouble or anything that may have jeopardized their housing situation.

My mother was a grafter, working right up to the time when she gave birth to me. Moving into the flat was an opportunity for my mum to work at home whilst looking after me in my first few months of life. Mrs. Kay did not want to lose my mother as a good employer so she was happy to provide my mother with homework, bringing cut material for mother to put together and make into garments. This continued until my mother left me with a child minder so she could return to work. The child minder was the mother of a friend who looked after me like her own. Mother would do a full twelve hour shift then took extra work home from the factory, carrying heavy bundles of cut material on her own whilst using public transport. She would then pick me up from the child minder before going home to start her second shift.

Mum rented a second-hand industrial sewing machine from her boss, then decided to buy one from Mrs. Kay and carried on working at home, putting the cut cloth bundles together and making dresses. Firstly, her mission was to pay for the sewing machine, then saving the money earned, to buy household items and build a home for her little family. My father, on the other hand, earned far less, worked fewer hours and spent most of his money on gambling and womanizing. My mother said that however much my father wasted his money, he was always a good provider and paid all the household bills. Dad was not a materialistic man. He was extremely simplistic, never wanting luxurious goods or understood why other people craved for them. He did introduce me to two things in life; God and Arsenal football club.

Father became a believer in Jesus Christ in 1966 when he heard Billy Graham preach in Earls Court Arena. He never did however, accept that he was a Christian but called himself a believer. I never fully understood why he did not accept the Christian tag but did trust and believe that he had faith in Jesus Christ and the resurrection and what was written in the Bible. He introduced me to God, indirectly from the age of five by taking me with him to worship in Chorley Hall, which was part of the London City Mission organisation, in Dalston, East London. Father read the Bible many times and confidently knew many of its chapters by heart. My mum though, never gave up her Muslim background, although she was not a strict practitioner of the faith but respected its rules and traditions.

It was a damp, dark, rainy evening on Monday, May 3, 1971, I remember my father coming home from work and doing something I never seen before. He was ardently trying to tune the family radio to listen to the commentary of a football match between Tottenham and Arsenal, playing at White Hart Lane. Then Ray Kennedy scored what was the winning goal which meant that Arsenal had won the 1970/71 English league 1st Division Championship. Not that I knew it at the time but it was apparently the moment that all Arsenal fans dreamt of; the moment when Arsenal would beat their arch enemy, North London rivals Spurs at White Hart Lane to win the League title. I remember the radio commentator shouting and The Gunners fans celebrating by invading the pitch of their North London rivals. Arsenal were League Champions! Dad jumped up in the air and started shouting with joy. Until that day, I did not even know that he had any interest in football or that he was even an Arsenal fan. When my father showed any interest in any sporting event, I always thought he had a bet on the final outcome. That night I surely did find out. The look of delight and happiness in his face immediately made me the Arsenal fan that I am now.

Dad's other real passion that I definitely inherited from him, was his love for food, well eating. He lived to eat. One of his loves that later life brought about was his fondness of Florida. He loved Orlando and I am sure the introduction of the concept of 'eat as much as you like' was the crucial reasoning of his love for the sunshine state. He liked Universal Studios and enjoyed seeing the life-size images of John Wayne on horseback in one of the rides in the theme park. My dad loved the old black and white films and knew of many that I had never heard of. He liked Marilyn Monroe, calling her the perfect woman. I don't think it was because she was blonde, as he did like all women! He told me that he thought she was murdered and that her life story showed that life was not like the movies. .

The Circumcision

In August 1967, mum and dad decided to go to back to Cyprus for a long break. For me it was my first holiday with my parents to go together to see old friends and relatives and to show their family that they were still on track with their 'Cypriot Dream'. As far as I can remember, this was their first holiday together - they did not go on honeymoon – and it had taken months of planning and years of savings. Once in Cyprus, we went to stay in Lefkara, my mother's home village. My granddad then decided why not have my circumcision party whilst I was there- everything was right for it including my age. My granddad was so happy to see his daughter come back home, he wanted the whole village to know this and to show her off. Preparations were soon underway; my granddad was the local butcher so lamb and chicken would be on the menu and lots of it. As usual we were going to feed the masses. Feeding others had always been a blessing to my parents, they loved it, and everyone ate and ate and then still took food home. When it was announced that Naci was going to have his day, everybody in the village would be invited and they would all come.

Those days were not renowned for health and safety or any kind of pain relief but I know that my father would have hired the best man for the job. I'm sure he was not a doctor but the most reputed in his field on the island. When other parents heard that a mohel was coming to the village, all young boys who needed to be circumcised asked to be done on that day.

So the day began, the mohel went on his rounds whilst in the area and left me to last. I had to follow the traditional day. I was dressed in the usual costume and looking back at old photos, I looked like a miniature Father Christmas without the white beard and bobble hat. I was then paraded on horseback on a big, overfed, tired looking mule. It was the closest thing to a horse in the village I suppose. The mule was escorted by the animal's owner around the village to the sound of drums and flutes, the family clapping, followed closely by the rest of the village behind, whistling. All I can remember is me being very scared, nervous not to fall off this overfed fly-infested imitation of a horse. I was also trying (unsuccessfully) to shut out the clapping and cheering behind me.

Before I knew what was happening I was snatched from my formal transport and rushed into the living room of my auntie's house. A single bed had been put into the place of where there was once a sofa. The room was crowded with guests, most of whom I did not know. They were all clapping, I looked at all these faces looking at me, laughing and smiling, some whistling. I was stripped of my red suite and my undergarments in a rush as if I was being raped. I was then forcibly robed in a white overall, like a NHS hospital gown but this one was made of silk. It looked like I was going down to theatre for a major operation. I couldn't understand what the rush was but then the horror show really began.

Two men picked me up, one on each side, one took my left arm, the other my right. They both lifted me into the air, split both my legs apart and this so called 'doctor' pulled the foreskin of the tip of my penis and with one blow CUT! I was circumcised. I screamed at the top of my voice! All I could do was look on the ground. I saw blood dripping like a tap onto the floor and into a container under me. The white robe quickly became saturated red. My two burly supporters then wrapped me with the robe whilst a third person was trying to catch the leaking blood under me into a sort of sacramental chalice. I was then quickly wrapped up tightly and put into my prepared bed.

The party then began for everyone else; not for me though. The pain in my groin was excruciating. I could hear the music from the other room and people enjoying the celebrations. Some were talking, others shouting and laughing. My penis was throbbing, burning as if someone had poured hot oil over it. It was bleeding and I was crying. I just curled up and made myself as small as I could, just lying in this bed. People started queuing up to congratulate me on how brave I had been. Most came with gifts, generally gold from the family, money from the more affluent, biscuits, nuts and fruit from others.

The healing then had to start and be allowed to take place. I was treated like royalty, literally wrapped in cotton wool. On the second day I was allowed to leave the bed and sit by a window. I watched the other boys who also were circumcised on the same day. They were playing football and all looked fine but it was about a week before I was allowed to walk on my own.

When the three of us all returned to London, I at the time could not foresee or visualise what was to be the beginning of my future and where my life was going. My father examined my 'operation' to check on how it was healing. He suspected that things were not as they should be. Again dad took me to the man he judged as the best available, a real doctor. Yes there was something wrong. I needed to be circumcised again, this time less barbarically, under surgical conditions and with no party. Fortunately the operation was a success. The doctor did though tell my mother that I was very obese for my age and that I needed to start to lose weight. They immediately put me on a strict diet. This was new to me and at the age of five, I weighed five stones (about 40kilos). I was told that I was too fat, needed to reduce what was I eating, change habits and to do more exercise. My new life had begun; a new mission. I remember the doctor trying to explain to my mother about diets. He told me that when I ate eggs, I should eat only the white of the egg and leave out the yolk. Well, I stopped eating the whites, for no other reason, than because I was not going to listen to the doctor's advice.

At that early age, I unconsciously decided I was not going to do this, as much as the consensus wanted me to lose weight it was them against me. It seemed that way, it has always been 'them and I' with my parents, with my friends, my family, work colleagues, or society on the whole. I never felt that I was part of them, I was always an outsider looking in, not part of them, not one of them. As the years went on, I single-mindedly decided I am not fat and was not going to lose any weight. There were days and occasions when I was reminded how fat I was, children would tell me, young people would laugh whilst looking at me, others would just look. These episodes would last for a few minutes and yes, they hurt, but the pain did not bother me enough to do anything about it. I would just blank it out of my mind and carry on.

I not only felt I was an 'outsider' looking in from that young age but also started noticing that I felt that I was invisible. Not physically but felt I was being overlooked and ignored by others most of the time. I was afraid of being noticed. I quickly learnt, that in order for someone to fit into a group, they need to possess certain qualities. I found it difficult to do the straightforward things, even 'life skills'. Living nervously, afraid of being judged, spending all my life walking on egg shells. This resulted in never being picked by teachers to do school things like the school football team, the choir, for a main part in the seasonal drama production or even as class monitor. It never ever happened to me, I was never considered. I felt that I really did not fit in. Eventually I was not confident at carrying out the simplest of tasks. In a way I started getting worried if I *was* picked for fear of embarrassing myself and wouldn't try things that were beyond my comfort zone for the fear of failing. I think this period was the start of me finding it difficult just to be accepted in society or a group.

I started becoming the clown of the group, making people laugh to get noticed. I found that being unconventional, a non-conformist, sometimes acting, the more ludicrous the better, got me some attention from others. I quickly learnt new survival techniques of pushing boundaries and finding ways to "get away with it" as I used to say. There were several aspects that separated me and made me this self- acclaimed outsider such as my lack of self-assurance but I also genuinely felt and believed I was this 'outsider, this invisible man'. I was not generally accepted or welcomed into what was going on, even in the playground. I just created my own agenda to alienate myself from 'them'. Physically I was definitely not unnoticed, not only was I putting on weight daily, the clothes I had no choice to wear, showed me up as well. They were all obviously made for an adult but crudely altered by my mother the dressmaker for me.

I remember always dreading the subject of needing to buy clothes and I always needed clothes as I quickly got too fat for what I was wearing. I used to wear out the bottoms of my trousers because I could not take the time to pull my trousers up. Going to clothes shops were very emotional and scary times; I would want to hide when we were in clothes shops. It was not only embarrassing for me, I also felt that my mother was ashamed too and I could feel her pain and hurting inside. She would express her frustrations by telling me in Turkish, in front of the shop assistant that I never listen to her when she talked about my eating. I knew that I could never find fitting trousers, or a shirt. I used to fear the new school terms, any family weddings or parties. My first memories of school life were that of the late 1960's early 1970's when again I wanted to be like the other children, especially when it came to fashion. Even now I still like to dress as well as I can. I remember in this period flared trousers were in fashion with side pockets just above the knee. My mother tried to make me happy, and did her best to buy me them but as usual getting a good fitting pair was impossible. The size of my waist was not normal, so a bigger size meant longer trousers, which needed a lot of shortening; with these alterations the shape of the flare was lost and the side pockets were too low and they sure did look odd. I now started to become fashion conscious and didn't like what I had to wear or the way I looked. I suppressed my self-consciousness and self-paranoia. But I liked food more.

My mother tried anything and everything, to make me lose weight and it soon developed into an obsession for her. However as much as she wanted me to be slim, I was not going to do it. I knew what my mother's weaknesses were and I started manipulating them. I would make up stories and lies about how one can lose weight, tell her I needed extra pocket money to pay for swimming or go to the gym. Even at that young age I invented fictitious saunas and plans that I needed to do that would benefit me and she believed me. I was only about eight or nine years old but exploited the circumstances that I now found myself in. I used the extra pocket money I had fraudulently gained to buy more junk food, sausage rolls and doughnuts being the most popular as they were readily available. I bought them regularly from the corner shop near my school to satisfy my needs or as treats for my peers to buy their friendship. This pattern continued well into my secondary school life. The family GP monitored my condition and advised my mother. He constantly told me that I needed to diet and my mother was going to do her best for me to lose weight. I was determined not to however and I think it was then that I unconsciously started to enjoy being that rebel that I have been for most of my life. At that age I was starting to hate the world, blaming it for putting me on a diet and later on, for giving me this body.

My mother would arduously prepare me colourful fresh salads and keep them moist by wrapping them and storing them in the refrigerator until dinner time. I would go home for dinners during school term. Walking home for lunch was meant to be additional exercise. She never knew that as well as the salad I would start with puff pastry wrapped sausage meat, a doughnut or two as my main course together with as many sweets and chocolate bars as I could afford. I remember one time my mother putting me on a lemon diet. A neighbour told her that drinking freshly squeezed lemon juice on an empty stomach first thing in the morning was meant to be a good fat burner. Mother told my father to buy extra lemons in the weekly shopping. She made the drink for me like clockwork before I woke up every morning. I never knew how many lemons she squeezed into this tea cup everyday but I was forced to drink it. I remember spending the rest of the day having stomach pains and cramps. Another time, the same neighbour told my mother that skipping with a rope was good exercise. I started to hate this neighbour, and dreaded it whenever he came to our house or spoke to my mother, getting fearful about what other ideas he had on me losing weight. My mum was so focused on my size that she would try anything. I would look at this man, and despise him not only because his ideas were causing me grief and embarrassments but also because he was short and plump himself, I soon was put on a skipping regime, twice a day morning and evening, on schooldays, and three times a day at weekends. Mum would call me into the centre of the living room, to skip for what felt like forever. For months I felt like a sloth bear forced to dance on hot coals. It did not matter who was there visiting our home. The ordeal was made worse by the fact I was often being watched by all my mother's coffee drinking neighbours. Whilst they were having a coffee and gossiping about each other, I was the centre of attention, skipping. I don't think I ever benefited from my mother's hard work or determination. This cycle of me exploiting the situation of my disease, trying to find money to finance my food addiction and buying the friendship of my peers carried on well into my teens.

My life in secondary school was mostly intolerable; at least it was mixed school. Having girls around made it bearable at times. Thinking of some girls, secretly liking them created a fantasy life that I only knew. The bad experiences though really dominated my time at Arnos Secondary. I spent the first three years trying to avoid ever having a shower after any physical education lesson or outside games. I then spent the last two years avoiding P.E and swimming altogether. This great fear of taking my clothes off and showering really took over and I completely lost focus on why I was meant to be at school. It all started with my first ever P.E. lesson. This was a complete shock to the system. After a ninety minute workout, we were expected to strip off and all get into the shower. In the 1970's showers consisted of a load of shower-heads fastened to the wall, all pointing downwards, with one tap that the 'Games' teacher controlled, switching the water on and off. This was definitely a first and once in a lifetime experience as this was my first and last time in the five years of attending Secondary School. I think the other boys and myself waited over ten minutes for the water to heat up but it never did. Some of them washed with no hesitancy, some had pretended to wash. Well, I didn't know what to do. I was only scared and worried about all the eyes watching me. As well as the problem with me stripping off naked and me having to endure a freezing cold shower, I had to endure those nasty comments and the loud different tones of laughter from other boys looking at my obese infested body and its development. I did not have the monopoly of these cruel and wicked jibes, other boys experienced taunts too but I only heard those directed at me. The one that hurt the most which still haunts me was being called "prick-less!" This name was not only limited to that shower time but followed me into the playground and classrooms and hurt more in the presence of girls. Questioning my manhood was the most demoralizing aspect. I now still get emotional when I think about all those excuses that I had to invent; so as avoid having a shower ever again or taking part in recreational games ever again. At the time it was all about avoidance, hiding and survival.

I needed to invent excuses daily to keep away from the showers. Such as I had forgotten my towel, or didn't have appropriate clothing. I started making up medical conditions such as incurable verruca or lifelong ear infections, all authourised by letters forged and signed by me pretending to be one of my parents. This all contradicted what they were hoping I was doing in school as my mum wanted me to as much exercise as I could. Whenever the school arranged trips away all my class mates would be thrilled and they all could not wait to bring the reply slips back and take up the limited spaces. In contrast I never worried about missing out; I was glad that there were these restrictions to places I knew I was not going. School trips which entailed staying overnight were the scariest ones. I made sure that the letters never got home and always signed the reply slips myself.

From that first year of secondary school, aged eleven, I started noticing girls. My first love was Helen Sawyer, a blonde, with blue eyes. At that age I knew what I liked. We were friends for five years but I never ever had the courage to ask her out because I was afraid of the rejection or losing her friendship. Helen never knew how much I liked her.

In 1976 my parents and I went to Cayirova in Northern Cyprus two years after the Turkish intervention on the island to end an ongoing conflict between the Greeks and Turks. Prompted by a Greek-backed coup d'état in July 1974, my mother's family were relocated in a previously Greek occupied village. I remember this holiday well, as this period was an anxious and nervous for everyone on the island as well as my parents. The war had devastated the island as well as creating a lot of uncertainty. My mother's youngest brother found a big stamp collection which must have belonged to someone who lived in the house that was given to my grandad by the Turkish authorities. My uncle generously gave me this collection as a gift. As a young teenager it gave me hope that the collection could be worth a small fortune. It started a hobby that I never had any interest in before. Once back in the UK I started buying other stamps, adding to my collection, reading and doing research on my collection. My uncle from my father's side found out about my collection when it came up in conversation. He talked about how he liked stamps and had thousands from all over the world. It became a talking point whenever we met. I never ever saw his collection, but he showed a lot of interest in mine, telling me that I had a lot of interesting stamps in my collection. One day he told me that he was going to a stamp collectors fair and if I wanted, he could take my collection to be valued. As a fourteen year old child I believed him. I never ever saw the stamp collection again. My uncle never ever told me of the stamps value or returned them,

In fact, my uncle did not ever mention the stamps again. I was too intimidated by him to ask. The reason I feel I need to include this matter as part of my story is mainly because I have never been able to forget it. At first I felt self-blame and feelings of shame and guilt. Over the years when I reflect on this abuse by my uncle on how he caused so much fear, terror and unsafe feelings. I know he will never know that the anger I have carried for years turned inward, and could be one of the contributory factors to depression,

In the same year my father bought his first retail business, a sweet shop. A chocolate- lover's dream? In the weekends I would go and work there helping him restock, serve customers and watch out for any shoplifting. This was another chance for me to eat and it gave me an opportunity to steal money out of the till. I had now also become a big thief; I was now stealing money from wherever and whenever I could to pay for my food dependency. If I could not steal money, I would take food, all high-calorie snacks, sneak it into the house and hide my fix. The second mission was getting the wrappers out of the house before my mother noticed. My guilty pleasure in life was eating the stolen chocolates bars from my dad's shop and hiding them in the odd places around the house. I would look to find an excuse to stay at home when my parents wanted to go out such as doing non-existent school homework. Once I was alone I could make myself a sandwich or eat from my hidden stash.

Secondary school days from the age of eleven till sixteen is a blur but the few incidents I do remember are certainly embedded in my head. French was a compulsory subject and I had a very old lady teacher, well, in the eyes of an 11 year old, she was old! Ms. Pixner was given the privilege of trying to teach me this new language. Her skills in controlling a class of school children could be questioned. She gave us all a French name and my given name was, I think, Neville. Whenever she greeted me or asked me any sort of question she would address me as Neville. I was not innocent and blameless as it was very easy to push boundaries with her. I think every lesson I shared with her, I was told to go into the stationary cupboard and stay there. I remember her sometimes locking the cupboard whilst I was in there. I am sure my claustrophobia started then. On bad days she would send me to the head of lower school, Mr. Cooper. Mr. Cooper would look at me when I entered his office after about my sixth visit. He would ask "Ms. Pixner?" I would nod, and he would tell me to go away. "Tell her you have seen me!" I would walk back with a smile on my face, thinking I had got one over the French teacher. 'Got away with it'. My disruptive, showing-off behavior was not only monopolized in French lessons. Library and media studies were also taught by a teacher that I loved pushing my luck with. Mrs. Stafford's patience and style were more laid back and on this occasion, I really pushed it. She had no choice but to send me to stand outside the class, instructing me to stay there until she called me back in. Whilst standing outside, my luck had run out as Mr. Cooper decided to walk past. He looked at me, and just asked "Ms. Pixner's class?" I told him it was not, in fact, it was Mrs. Stafford's class. He then told me to follow him. We went into his office. Before I knew it, Mr. Cooper was holding an old rubber plimsole. He told me to hold out my hand. After the first whack, I thought that was it. I then counted five more, thinking six of the best. However, my ordeal did not stop there, I could feel my hand throbbing, burning and stinging. The whacking continued, Mr. Cooper started groaning and jumping up and down building up the energy to whack me harder. By then, I was in pain never experienced. I'm sure he hit me more than the twelve that it was rumored that he had punished others. "Now go back to your class, boy!"

I remember running to the class, entering the room and Mrs. Stafford saying she wasn't ready to allow me in yet. I ignored her and sat down in my seat. She looked at me, saw that I was crying and came over to me. She looked at my eyes. I looked down at my hand which was now swollen and glowing red. She looked, also asking what had happened and I told her. She replied quietly that was not what she wanted to happen. I couldn't forget this experience. Iit took me many months to get over but I have never been able to get rid of the scar left in my head. I had to cover my hand from my parents for a long time, as I believed that they would not accept that this was not right. I was the one in the wrong, the one who deserved what I got.

Another pivotal point in my school days was that time of the year when it was our class form's turn to do the annual school play, in front of the whole school and the public. My part was very minimal; I was one of those other kids who were only there because we had to be seen to be included. I was a non-speaking tree, made by me in the art lessons wearing these stuck-on paper branches standing in the background of a forest scene, dancing onto the stage standing there for about 30 seconds and attempting to wobble off stage. The school invited all the parents but I chose not to tell mine. However my mother heard the news from all the neighbours whose children where part of the production, one way or another. Obviously, I did not bring the invitation letter home for my parents to come and watch their son. My mother asked me if I was in the play and I told her that I only had a very small part. Mum was so happy and insisted that she wanted to come and see me in my great role. When she did she came on her own of course, dad couldn't, but wouldn't have if he could have. My mum was concerned that all my peers were a lot taller than me. She even asked if the other children were older than me. I told her that actually, I was a lot older than most of them.

She was that worried that she took me to our doctor who referred me to an Endocrinologist. After many tests, it was established that I had many illnesses because I had an under active pituitary gland. They discovered that I had stopped growing and that my physical and sexual development was very retarded. I remember one condition which was called Gonadrophinism, which was a form of dwarfism. After further tests, they prescribed me a very expensive course of growth hormones injections. *(Growth hormone treatment refers to the use of growth hormone (GH) as a prescription medication—it is one form of hormone therapy. Growth hormone is a peptide hormone secreted by the pituitary gland that stimulates growth and cell reproduction. In the past, growth hormone was extracted from human pituitary glands and was later made artificially).* Rumour had it that later side effects may cause a human version of Mad Cow's Disease. So I don't know if I will be mad later on. Some would argue I already was." This course entailed three injections into my bottom, three times weekly.

The treatment continued until my bones had fused and there was no more space for any more growth. This would be the main and most important factor in my new life for over three years. This life-changer brought many consequences. I needed to go to my GP three times a week, sometimes waiting over an hour in the waiting room for the doctor to administer the drug. Seeing my doctor almost every other day, I started asking him questions about my future and the consequences of my illness. I was about thirteen years old and listened to every word he told me. Some I understood, other answers were too confusing and sophisticated. I do remember though, much of what he

29

said. The hardest one to swallow was the one that it would be unlikely that I could have children or even a normal sex life. Now I started being very self-conscious and my paranoia could not have got any deeper about anything to do with sex and relationships as well as my other issues. Often the doctor was complacent on how he would administer the drugs. Sometimes I did not even have to pull my trousers down for the injection. The doctor would be so busy, he would just take a lucky shot and stick the sharp needle into me and I would walk out of his surgery. Often I could feel that I was bleeding, or the drug was excreting back out. I would then walk down the High Road to the local betting shop where my dad was to get a lift home. Dad would be making his last minute bets on that evening's greyhound racing or that night's football matches. This was a must after his day at work, a ritual for him. This meant more waiting for me. Sometimes I was outside the betting shop for more hours on that wintry cold night. On some occasions, the manager of the betting shop felt sorry for me and let me stay and stand in the doorway. I started to get curious and found a taste for gambling. I quickly learned about betting and enjoyed the buzz. I blame this period for giving me that appetite for gambling.

Whenever I visited my hospital consultant for checkups or follow ups I asked him the same questions that I asked my GP and told him what my doctor had said. He assured me that the doctor's opinion was to be respected but was not necessarily right, there were lots of treatments available for almost all of my ailments and things were improving daily with new drugs, techniques and a better understanding of my illness. He did, though, remind me that nothing in life was guaranteed. I was told I needed further tests and these tests would be ongoing all my life. On odd days like Christmas, and bank holidays when my doctor's surgery was closed, a district nurse had to visit my home to administer my usual injection. This was witnessed by whoever was visiting our home, so it was then that all sorts of rumors started about me. I was a diabetic, I had kidney disease even that I was dying because of some incurable illness. The most poignant comment for me was that I would never have children. At the time I did not know these rumors would come back again and again to haunt me.

The Growth Hormone Therapy Treatment was revolutionary at its time and I quickly became a sort of celebrity in my school. My art teacher designed a growth chart in the classroom and this was the highlight of my art lessons, each week, visibly seeing my progress I grew about 15 inches (40cm) throughout the duration of the treatment. Aside from this, my school days were not happy ones. The feeling of inferiority with my peers continued and acting the clown was becoming an art form. I smiled all the time so that nobody knew how I felt, because laughing was a mask that hid what I truly felt inside. I found myself needing to show off more and more, in order to keep up this charade. I did this by being over generous with spending and buying for my peers so that they would be my friends. This had become an everyday way of life for me and to finance this I had to find ways to make the money. I also needed money to pay for my own over eating habits. Stealing money, conning my poor naive mother, shoplifting, had all become part of my survival techniques.

I left school, with the minimum qualifications, attaining only the minimum entry requirements, just enough to be able to get into college to do an 'O' Level course. In those days, you needed a minimum of five good 'O' Levels to qualify to do an 'A' Level course and needed at least two 'A' Levels to be able to enter university. My ambition at the time was to go onto University to study law. I cannot ever remember if anyone told me that I was being over ambitious but if someone did, I obviously was not listening. So I needed to start doing the appropriate course to achieve my aim. College life was just a further extension of school for me, nothing had changed, except that now I could now wear any clothes, even if they did not fit properly. Looking odd was cool in college, as you were licensed to be rebellious. At College, I started to realize my immaturity and what a sheltered life I had led.

I found myself being very anti- social, avoiding gatherings of other students like the college bar, where my peers would talk about everything, from politics, music, drugs to social history. I could not relate to any of it. Never heard of punk, or Led Zeppelin or the Tudors. Even going to the canteen with my classmates did not happen. I was nervous eating with others in crowded spaces as I was afraid in case I spilled food down my front. I would hide in the library whenever there were no lessons. Not reading or studying, actually, I was mostly sleeping or acting the clown. In the classroom, things were no different. I was spending almost all the time trying to make people laugh by being absurd and doing outrageous things like a spoilt child pushing boundaries.

During this period I passed my driving test and my parents bought and insured a car for me. It was an incentive for me to stay on at college and study but I used the car as somewhere else to hide. I would often buy myself a take away then drive the car to a secluded spot and eat my food on my own. I would use up free times on my timetable on my own where I knew no one was seeing whatever I was doing. My life continued to be made of fraudulent behaviors, a smoke screen used to cover over my insecurities and feelings of being inadequate. From the outside, I tried to appear proud and happy. I possessed many things that others of a similar age would have envied, such as money and a car. What most people did not know, however, that inside it was a very different scenario. Most of the showing off was me saying, "Are you noticing me?" If only they knew how I really felt, unnoticed or unrecognized. I felt that I did not get the respect that I deserved as a human being and so, me showing off and being loud was the message of my behavior, "I am here, please notice me!" I would often worry about other people's opinions about me. I believed they knew more about life than I did, so because they were more experienced than me I assumed they were right and I was wrong.

College life had become very monotonous, mostly because I did not work or study hard enough. I spent six years in college playing 'catch up,' learning life skills that should have come naturally, but however much I tried, I felt my size held me back. The expectation of the course I had enrolled into was that a student should achieve five 'O' Levels in one year and progress onto the 'A' Level course which was for a further two years. During this period P was born. After nineteen years of being the only child, I now had a little sister. Well, she was not really a sister. In my mind, I felt I was just another father for her. Not a mature father, she was just a daughter born to love and to give love back. I remember when I was in the hospital maternity unit, waiting for her to be born, there were other anxious people who were waiting for their loved ones to give birth too and thought that I was a father in waiting.

I should have achieved university entrance in three years. I really struggled and did not pass the required 'O' Levels needed in the first year, in fact, it took me three years to get on to the 'A' Level course and it took me a further three years before I felt I was ready to take my first exams. It was expected that university applications should have been submitted well before these were taken. Well, as expected, I

33

read the appropriate university prospectuses, chose the five that I had to choose, not because it was a good university, or it was near my home, or that it ticked the right boxes, simply I chose those that I liked the sound of. I was never advised otherwise and no teacher asked me what I was doing. As usual, I was left to my own devices to find my own way. I submitted the single form to UCAS, the Universities Selection Body who was supposed look at the form pass on my details to my selected university. One by one the universities were supposed to offer me a place in their establishment unconditionally, offer me a place if I achieved the right grades in my exams or offer me an interview if they wanted to know more about me. Well, I must have been the first student in the whole college who got replies, back from them all, and the quickest. UCAS sent me a slip of paper with all of my five selected Universities printed on it. By each one, the side was the word REJECTED, in red capitals. I looked at that word, swallowed the saliva in my mouth and just told myself; "I hate that word!" Seeing the word written five times in a row, made me feel so alone and rubbish. The universities did not know me, or how I was going to do in my exams! This was no different from my experiences over the past nineteen years. I felt insignificant, worthless.

M

The first time I ever met M was the week-end that I received my 'A' Level results. The brown envelope arrived on Saturday morning and my parents did not like the information it contained. I had failed abysmally. That weekend was very significant however, in that it was the start of a twenty year emotional mental merry-go-round. It was a Sunday evening in August 1983, a day after my parents' disappointment and I felt more or less forced to feel ashamed whereas in reality, I felt sorry for myself. I chose to stay in my bedroom that day, reflecting and analyzing the situation, wondering how I could turn this situation into a positive. I was confident in myself that I would find a way out of this. My mother would shout exaggeratedly and show her frustrations but experience told me that she would get over it. People usually took their 'A' Levels at the age of eighteen, I was twenty-one. What was my next move? I could hear my mother's voice from the living room downstairs explaining to visitors why she was angry and frustrated. Guests had been popping in all day to come to see my aunty who had come from Cyprus to stay with us from Cyprus. I did not know any of them. My mother told them angrily how much she had sacrificed for me to study and what had happened. She told them how useless I was, what an ungrateful son I was and that I was Eshek' (ass). My emotional state and self-pity was being interrupted by the footsteps of these people coming upstairs to use the bathroom. Then M popped her head around the door which was ajar, and asked was I Naci? I nodded, she invited herself into my room and told me that "everyone's talking about you downstairs". She introduced herself, telling me she was eighteen and a hairdresser. She then climbed on my bed and started to jump up and down. I thought this was the funniest thing I had seen for a long time. The situation was so surreal. I unashamedly fell in love with M there and then; love at first sight. Who was this girl? She was like an angel sent from the heavens above, guided down to come into my life at this low time. I was seriously and quickly besotted for the first time in my life. First time I wanted to seriously know who this girl was. Two days later my dreams were crushed, when my aunty (who had known her parents for years) told me that M was only fifteen and still at school. Although I was over 20 years old, I had never been in love or even had a girlfriend, or even been this close to a girl. Those forty or so minutes in my bedroom had changed my life. I wanted to marry this girl NOW! I did not care what the consequences were or what I had to do. I was willing to wait until she was sixteen. M had an older brother and I soon became friends with him to become closer to her. She never realized what a spell she had on me. Eventually, and bravely, I told M how I felt about her. M's mother was very down to earth and easy to talk to and she had sensed my intentions. I quickly started calling her mum and we all became friends. I immediately put myself on a diet. I had never thought of losing any weight until then. I completely stopped eating. It was the longest time I had been on a strict diet and I was starving myself. I had completely lost any appetite I had, so it was easy. I think it was the most weight I have ever lost since I was five.

M's Mother was a close friend of my aunty so she soon got to know about the situation. On one of the days when I visited M's house, her mother said that she wanted to talk to me. She tried to let me down gently by telling me that M loved me like a brother rather than in any other way. M would not know how much she meant to me, or how devastated I was when her mum said that that her daughter did not want to marry me. The next thing she said was heartbreaking and left me traumatized. They had heard from others that I could not father children. I remember the day as if it was yesterday. What was worse in the back of my head was it could have been true. Was this the reason I had been unwanted, rejected? I felt that lump quickly coming back and growing in my throat, I wanted to cry. I held the tears back as long as I could, feeling that my masculinity was being questioned, once again. It was not the time to cry. I remember starting to babble and try talking my way out of the situation. I desperately wanted to hold on to what I had with M. Only I knew how much I loved her. I started lying and said that I had already fathered a child. I was so anxious and nervous I would have said anything. She continued to say that M was not ready to get married. She was planning to go to college and become a hairdresser. M's mother kept on apologizing on behalf of her daughter, saying that her house would always be open for me. I remember leaving M's home for the last time and getting in my car, driving around the corner and just bursting out in tears.

I do not think I will ever get over the break up with M, even now, over 30 years after the first day I met her. Always I'm asking myself, what if? M will never know; she was too young, innocent and blameless at the time. Maybe on reflection, this is why I still have some feelings for her. She was my real first love. M did, however, unconsciously motivate me to continue with my education and I started a course to train as a legal executive, which was another pathway to qualify and practice law. Soon after the break up, I even thought to myself that if there was a slight chance of me ever marrying M, becoming a solicitor would be a good start.

U

Paradoxically it was this period that my father reminded me that he was dying and wanted to see me married first. Father randomly mentioned this subject but now was talking about this more constantly. Fate foretold that one day when mum and dad went out to visit a friend, they lost their way and whilst trying to find a certain road spotted a man tidying and cleaning an ice cream van parked on a driveway, in one of the streets. My dad approached him to ask for directions. Father recognized the man who happened to be an old friend of my parents who they hadn't seen for years. He invited them into his home for a coffee and a catch up chat. This was an opportunity for my father to brag about his son and advertise, to tell the whole world that I was ready for marriage. Coincidently the man's niece was in the UK and was an ideal candidate. The situation was perfect, I am sure both parties were enthusiastic to link the two of us up.

I think this was the last day that my dad physically hit me, not that he was an abusive or violent man but it did happen. When my parents came home, I was outside standing on the corner of the road, where our house was. I was with other youngsters who lived in the area. When I saw the car pulling up I walked over to them, my mother was taking care of my baby sister, dad was looking at me and smiling, and then he looked at me up and down. I remember I was very scruffily dressed, had long messy hair, was unshaven and had not bathed for a long time. He asked me, with a disgusted look, "Is this the man that I'm trying to find a wife for?" I quickly answered back, "Who asked you to look for a wife for me?" Before I knew it, Dad punched me in the head as hard as he could. I remember falling and feeling dazed. Once everything calmed down, I was told that I had been found a wife; all I knew then was that she was twenty-five and from Cyprus. Her name was U. She did not have a regular Turkish name, so I had trouble remembering it. Maybe this was a sign, but who listens to signs, or follows 'gut feelings'? I did not, I was too much of a coward to say no. I was too complacent to worry if things did not work out. Did I have any real choice? No. My life was now planned out. I was to be married off

My cousin was getting married in a fortnight and it was an opportunity for my intended and I to see each other. The ice cream man and his wife were invited to the reception. I was still in mourning over my break up with M, so nothing would have or could have stopped me thinking about her. I was in a 'Zombie state', mentally I was numb. Thinking about it now this sounds so sad. But I definitely was not in control of myself and the situation at that time.

The day of the wedding came and I saw for the first time the person who was going to be my future wife. I was inwardly anesthetized so all that I could remember of that first meeting was that she was a wearing a white dress. Reflecting back, she did not deserve this either as this could have been as scary for her as it was for me. It was such a cruel situation for us both in a way. I knew personally that I did not have any control of the circumstances, mentally or physically. One thing we both would agree on was that we were hoping it would have ended better than it did. At that time if someone had shown me an old lady of ninety-five I would probably have said yes to marrying her. My dad harassed me impatiently that evening to give me opinion, and blindly, to satisfy him and to get him to leave me alone, I told him that I liked what I had seen. The news from the other side was that this lady had liked me also, although she felt that I looked rather young. I was about twenty-three years old but I still had my boyish looks of which

I was very proud. Maybe it was the consequences of my hormone imbalance I suppose.

Everything started to move so quickly. Before I got to know anything about U, or became fully aware of what was happening, we were invited to the ice cream man's house as a family to formalize the arrangement and to be officially recognized as a couple, now waiting to be married. Traditional speeches took place. Dad asked his future daughter-in-law whether she was happy to be part of his family. She nodded, and shyly smiled and said: "Kismet", (whatever fate was written). I do, though, remember my arrogant and uncaring attitude when my father asked me the same question. I just wanted to get the situation to be over and done with as soon as possible. I just looked up at the ceiling. My attitude was I had to marry someone, so why not accept this woman who was willing to marry me? Before, I knew it or had any time to get over the break up with M I was forced to move on at someone else's pace and get ready for marriage.

I decided to conform to everything asked of me. I remember my Dad bragging about how studious I was training to be a solicitor. I was now engaged. We needed to get married quickly, as U's UK visa was running out and this was an easier option than me marrying her in Cyprus and getting a visa for her to return to the UK. This way was easier for everyone. The family got together and six months later we had an engagement party to declare our engagement.

The first few months of our engagement were quite nice. Even before the wedding reception, we seemed to be good together, enjoying each other's company. Although I was not in love with her, from early on I believed that eventually I would have fallen in love with her. U liked the theatre and musicals, so we often went and saw shows in the West End.

I remember one day when U went shopping to buy shoes but then lost the left one on the bus. When she arrived home, she was crying. I felt sorry for her and we went back to the shop together. I told her that I would go into the store and shoplift another one. She was not at all nervous. I found the appropriate shoe, took it off the shelf, and then put it into my bag. When we walked out of the store, U seemed happy, but the only problem was that I had stolen a right foot! U now had a pair of shoes, but they were for the same foot. After we had a laugh about my stupidity, U had the courage to go back into the store, with the purchase receipt and blamed the store for selling her two shoes that were not a pair.

We seemed to have grown as a couple and it was smoother and easier to start accepting the situation and become friends.

We arranged a small party to celebrate our marriage. It was going to be a quick marriage in a registry office, on a Monday, so most of my family could attend. Mondays were the day when most of them would have closed their fish and chip businesses so there would have been no problem for them all attending. Interestingly, about two days after I got married, M telephoned me, telling me that she had heard about my marriage as her mother had told her, I assume as my aunty had told her! M sounded angry, which was quite odd and I could not understand why she rang or was irritated. I still, to this day, cannot work it out.

Oddly, exactly one year after getting married in the Registrar's Office, we finally had our wedding reception. For that year leading up to our wedding reception, U and I continued to get to know each other and preparing for the wedding party was a major distraction from other matters. As usual, I was not going to do things in a conventional way. I did not want to have my wedding in the usual Cypriot banqueting Halls, though I honestly do not know why, I just wanted to do it my way. I found a nice wedding hall in Edgware that I had never heard of. I had no choice but to employ the usual Turkish wedding caterers, as they knew the expected cuisine. To complicate matters, London had experienced snow blizzards for three days before the wedding, so there were worries about how many guests would make an effort and turn up. My parents also were concerned about people finding the hall that I chose because of my stubbornness.

U and I arrived in a hired white Rolls Royce at the Hall at about 7.00pm that Sunday evening after spending most of the day getting ready and taking photos at the studio. My dad met me downstairs and told me not to come in yet, as only half the guests had arrived. I started to get worried - I had messed up again? Whilst sitting in the car in silence, waiting for the go-ahead to come in to the party, worry and boredom got the better of me. I started becoming the clown again like a child, lowering and raising the car window nearest me. Opening it up to the frozen, dry wind outside, U complained of the cold, but who was listening? I did a good job of also annoying the now, impatient chauffeur. After about the fifth or sixth time, the window decided not to rise up, the wind soon took over and the car became very cold. I could see the driver looking at us through his mirror, whilst U told me off, like a mother telling her child that he was naughty as I pressed the switch on the door vigorously. I thought to myself, in this farcical situation, "this is a Rolls Royce, not very efficient is it?" and the window's operating switch broke. The temperature inside the vehicle became unbearable for U. By then the driver had left his position and was trying to raise the window manually. He managed to do this, angrily telling me to leave the buttons alone. The situation was ended by my father coming and telling me that the caterers were getting impatient and that food needed to be served. We had waited as long as we could and I felt that the chauffeur had by now had enough of my company, so it was time.

When U and I entered the banqueting hall I thought I would have been nervous but seeing so many decorated empty tables took any anxiety I had, away. Tradition then demanded that when the marrying couple came into the arena, they had to dance a slow dance together. Well for me, it was us holding each other and U leading me around the dance floor. I had never done anything like this before. I don't think I had ever danced in my life. Any thoughts of how this looked, or me being embarrassingly bad at dancing were overshadowed by me looking at each empty seat as I passed it. Then both of us sat at a specially prepared table, but all I did for that first hour was look at the entrance of the hall to watch people coming in. I was praying for the invited guests to come at the start, then I started praying for them to stop coming. The bad weather and the guest's unfamiliarity of the venue had delayed a lot of them. My parents were well liked by many people and most of those who were invited were their friends, who had children who would be getting married in the future. Everyone invited came as a kind of loyalty gesture.

We used the money that we collected in gifts as a deposit to buy a house, which we planned to rent out. I was still studying and it was agreed that for the time being, we would both stay with my parents. I wanted to spend the money collected at our wedding on a honeymoon, but that wasn't the Turkish way at the time so it was a joint decision to invest in our future.

Smith's & Harry's

After successfully completing a year at college, I needed to find a job placement or even a full time job in the field of law, to enable me to continue my second year of the course. I applied to a lot of solicitor practices and a few Government Agencies. The Home Office responded first, inviting me for an interview. When I told my father that I had a chance to work for the British Home Office, he laughed and said in a posh English accent "The Home Office will never employ you, they only take Smiths and Harrys". My immediate reaction was to bet him that they would even though deep down I did feel that he did have a point. I felt I was not good at expressing myself and the thought of an interview scared me. As usual, I was angry with him and I had taken it personally. I felt that once again he was undermining me. Actually, my dad was really trying to stress that he believed that the Home Office was part of a racist establishment. I bet him £5 that I would get the job. The job was that of an AA which basically meant an Administrative Assistant. I felt that it was beneath me, though my dad did not know that. He commented that "if you get the job I will be delighted to lose the bet." I did get the job. Subject to a medical and felt a great sense of achievement despite knowing I could not continue with my Legal Executive course, because it was not in a legal department. I was not going to tell anybody, and no one would have been any the wiser.

The job had great prestige amongst those who knew me. "Naci worked for the Home Office! Wow!" Money did not come into it. The fact was I was working for the Home Office! After the briefest of medicals and a warning from the medical examiner that he had concerns about my weight and that might be complications in the future such as diabetes, he was going to pass me. My first Home Office post was with the Criminal Injuries Compensation Board in Goodge St, central London.

My first day was like my first day at school. I decided to wear one of my best suits, actually, it was the one I had worn for my engagement party. My mother made me a packed lunch and U had made sure that I was showered and was wearing clean underwear and even combed my hair for me. I followed the direction on my letter to get there and arrived two hours early. A Black security guard was on duty at the door of 19 Alfred Place SW1. I did not enter the building. I could see from the outside that he was sitting in behind a glass desk reading a newspaper. I had found the place, so decided to walk around and become familiarised with the area. The café and shops around my new workplace were still preparing for their daily openings. I treated myself to a cup of sweet tea, rewarding myself for getting a job with the British Government. I sat in a green communal area on one of the wooden park benches donated by a Mrs. Taylor in 1971 inscribed "in loving memory of my husband who worked here 1949-70". I ate Mum's packed lunch - she certainly knew how to make a good sandwich. Well, that was the first fifteen minutes used up, what was I going to do for the next hour or so? Then I discovered the worst thing that I could have I found; an amusement arcade, full of fruit machines. At first sight, I was delighted and happy. I remember going and finding that there was only one other punter in there, playing on a machine. He did not notice me watching him, he was too engrossed. There was a lady wearing a tight fitting, sky-blue FILA tracksuit-style hoodie with matching bottoms which were slightly faded, having obviously been washed more times than the top. What attracted me to her was her bleached bottle-blonde hair that needed the roots done. She had half a dangling cigarette in her mouth that she was puffing at, whilst trying to vacuum the stale smelling carpet laid on the arcade floor. The vacuum cleaner did not look healthy either, it had different kinds of coloured adhesive tape around parts that were obviously broken. I noticed that not all the fruit machines were switched on. One of them had 'Beware -broken glass' written over it and I guessed someone may have lost their money and lashed out. It felt strange going into the amusements that time of day, especially in a suit. I remember losing all the money I had in my pocket that morning. When I walked out, I just shrugged my shoulders, thinking that I had my return ticket home, I did not need any lunch and I was not hungry. Also I would be getting paid at the end of the month. I was very used to this position of losing all of my money this way and being penniless, so what was new? In the long run, I found out that having an Amusement center around the corner from where I worked was not good.

I walked to my workplace. When I got there I was taken to my section by Ola, the security guard and doorman, who had a very strong African accent. Although slightly unshaven, he looked immaculate. He was obviously proud of his looks, the uniform and his role. While in the lift to the 5th floor I gathered that he was coming to the end of his shift. He did twelve hours from 10pm the previous night. He took me to room no 5.1. It had a silver name plate screwed into the door on which was written 'Miss Angela Ruth Strauss, Senior Executive Officer'. I quickly noticed what her initials spelled and smiled to myself, Ola knocked on the door and immediately walked in without waiting for a reply. In a regimental style, he introduced me to this very skinny, small freckled woman behind an overcrowded desk on which I saw a cactus plant, four or five coffee mugs and a collection of odd owl-like ornaments. She thanked Ola and randomly started talking to him about her finding where they sold poppy seed cake. Ola just smiled and shook his head. He then left. Angela looked me up and down. I felt that she

46

was not impressed. She started to talk to me in a very posh English northern accent. She told me that her name was Angela, not Ange, or Angel. I didn't like her. I didn't know why except maybe due to the fact she was my boss. After the first 3 minutes of her attempt of induction, I switched myself off. I don't remember a thing she said apart from her being a senior officer of Her Majesty's Home Office responsible to Section 5. All I remember was the feeling of confusion and anxiety at the same time. As I had stopped listening to her introduction to 'Section 5' I did not have a clue what they did there and what I was supposed to do. She then told me to follow her next door into room 5.2. That was logical, I thought. She then showed me my desk by looking at it and bowing her head towards its direction, a the same time informing everyone in the room in a rushed tone, "Morning, section 5, this is Naki". Looking at me she continued, "Have I pronounced that right, Naki?" "No", I replied softly, with my dry mouth, "the C is a Gee, its Turkish, Nagee!" "Well, this is Nageeee! Our new long awaited AA, I'm sure you will all welcome him!" She then spoke in the direction of a young man, "Can I leave Nagee to you, Pete?" She then rushed out of the room, talking faster as she was leaving ... "got a 9.55 meeting with Quincy Russell QC. And we all know Quincy doesn't like to wait, don't we? Thanks, Pete!" I watched Pete acknowledge her by nodding his head and arrogantly saying nothing. I just looked at my desk in the middle of the room. I could not hide anywhere. I was now the center of attention, surrounded by filing cabinets.

In all four corners were desks with Executive Officers sitting in front of them with two other desks facing each other, where Administrative Officers were supposed to sit. Some of their seats were empty so there were thirteen of us in section 5, plus Angela. Pete got up from his desk by then and started to introduce me to the team in Section five, apologizing for those not present. I met the other Admin and Executive Officers. My first thought was that I am an Admin Assistant, the lowest rank in this hierarchy. I was the assistant to all twelve of them. This was not good. Pete was to be my immediate line manager. I read his full name from his name tag, Peter Roy Knight. I thought to myself that was odd, the first two people I have met in the morning have initials that spelled words, one was an ARS and the other was a PRK. I must have been really bored! I had been there for less than an hour.

Pete was a young 'cocky' graduate whose official post was Executive Officer with responsibilities. Yes, I was responsible to him. I think we were about the same age but that was all we had in common. He was obviously someone who prided himself on healthy living. He worked out, He told me that he was my boss, my supervisor. He would be teaching me anything I did not know and giving me the daily duties that needed to be done and writing my appraisals. That day I think was the first and last time that Angela and I ever spoke to each other apart from an occasional good morning if our paths crossed. Rumor had it that she was a morning person, who would have long liquid lunches. No-one in the office could ever remember seeing her being sober in an afternoon. Apparently, I should try and avoid her, if I ever saw her after 1.00 o'clock in the afternoon. Her nickname was the Spinster, from Jekyll and Hyde.

At first, the relationship between me and Pete was one of intimidation. He was not only my reporting officer, but he was also loud and very confident in himself, as well as being a very clever 'player' in the section we represented. He had established himself and knew his position well. We shook hands and he told me to "get comfortable" in my desk and asked me if I was happy with the desk and seat. I told him I will let him know once I had tried it. He didn't respond to my reply.

The first minute I sat at my desk I knew I was not going to be there for long. I felt that I was overdressed. Everyone was well dressed, but I was the only one in a suit. The AA in a suit? I asked myself and grinned inwardly. There was no routine or organized lunch times, everyone took whatever time they wanted, minimum thirty minutes each day. We were on a flexi-time scheme, working between 7.30am till 6.30pm daily, anything over seven hours twelve minutes. One could work a minimum of three hours thirty-six minutes daily or the maximum ten hours and thirty minutes.   Any extra hours would be built up as flexi-time and one could use the built-up time to take days off.   The first month I saw and felt Pete's nasty side. He was very chauvinistic and rude, often calling me names such as fat man, or "Mr. Nazi." One day I saw him coming back into the building at 6.30pm in the evening. He was also clocking out the same as me but he had already said goodnight to all of us at 3.45pm. When he clocked out I noticed the red light flash on the clock, which indicated that he clocking out. Pete also saw that I had seen the red light. He then quickly said out loud, "yeah I came back because I thought I had forgotten to clock, out Mate!" I just looked at him smiled and replied, "That's O.K. Mate!" We had become mates, all of a sudden. I then quickly told Pete my name and I gave him my hand in offer of a handshake and reminded him,"My name was Naci and not Mr. Nazi or Fat man". He obliged by nodding his head like he always did, took my hand and shook it. Our 'friendship' had begun.

In that month of my first job, I had heard that M had got engaged to a young lad in very random circumstances. My mum and dad were working as usual in the café that they owned in Woolwich, when a young couple came into the shop, enquiring if dad was considering selling the business. It was M and her fiancé. My Mum instantly recognized M, but my dad was none the wiser. Whilst M's young fiancé was talking to my father, M told my mother that she was now engaged and that her fiancé, who was only seventeen years old himself, grew up in South East London. Apparently, M asked about me and how my married life was going. When my mother came home that evening she secretly told me of what had happened that day, without U hearing any of the conversation. My immediate thought to myself was of slight jealousy and bitterness. Her fiancé must have been a better-looking boy than me! I asked myself, what happened to M's dreams of wanting to become a hairdresser?

Later on, about month after hearing that M had got engaged, my mother heard that her father had been killed in a road accident. When I received this tragic news I knew that it would have been hard for me to go and see M and her mother, especially with her fiancé being there but felt I needed to show my condolences and respect. I went to M's house with my father and M and I met and spoke very briefly. She loved her father and was obviously very shaken and broken. She told me that she thought this was God's way of punishing her. She asked me if I knew that she was going to get married in the next two weeks and I just shook my head, I did not know. She said that God was punishing her and that she will never be a bride, or wear her bridal gown, because of the horrible thing she had done to me. I just told her she was talking nonsense and that I had moved on. I just reminded her that it was just not written. When my father and I left the house, I just thought to myself what a liar I was; I had not moved on at all.

Working in CICB became easier after that evening, when I met Pete, 'fiddling the flexi' and cheating the clocking in system. I was in my element; by accident I discovered that I was the only one on the fifth floor who used the disabled toilet. The cleaner did not even bother cleaning it as he thought that it was never being used. The department used it as a store room for things that were never going to be used again. There were things in there that would have been classed as antiques, such as old typewriters. I never told anyone what I used it for but it was not as a toilet, it was my little hideaway and I even slept in it when I needed a little ten minute snooze. I would take fresh toilet rolls from the normal cubicles and build up stocks in my hideaway, using the softness of the toilet rolls as pillows to rest my head whilst sleeping. I always took the new toilet rolls, if the seal had not been broken it was mine. I soon made it my own. I remember taking all the fresh toilet rolls one morning, and whilst I was stacking them like a bricklayer building a wall around my secret room, a colleague from my section, called Joe, came into the public toilet. I quickly closed my door and he never knew I was in there. He went into one of the cubicles, where I had already taken the toilet rolls. I started hearing Joe grunting and doing his business and when he discovered that there was no paper, he got up, pants and trousers at his ankles, trying to hop to the next cubicle. I quickly opened the door of out of the cubicle I was hiding in, he looked at me, and I looked at him. Then he rushed into the next cubicle. I went back to my section and told Peter what happened. When Joe came back, into the section he looked at me and Pete, he knew that I had told him. I named my room the P.O. - Private Office. I even hung pictures of Arsenal football players on the walls. Pete became aware of my room, but just laughed at my cheekiness, and was amazed at how I took risks and pushed boundaries. In any case, he was my 'mate'.

Being an AA (Administrative Assistant) for the British Home office felt like it was the most monotonous job ever created, especially in the late 1980's when computers were not widely used. It was very paper orientated, involving lots of filing, cross referencing and more filing. I began to hate it more by the day. The fact that once again I felt undervalued, made me hate the whole concept of the establishment and I had to entertain myself to keep sane. I did this by once again acting the clown and becoming mischievous. I was now almost twenty-five years old but acted like a child. I remember one ordinary day, as I came out of my Private Office, I came across Spence, whose real name was Spencer but everyone called him Spence. He was a fellow AA who worked in the Accommodation Department. He was very thorough and one time refused to give me a new biro because I had lost the one he had given me a week ago, since I could not prove that I had used all the ink in my last one. Spence was distributing new stationery to all the sections. The stationary was all stacked and organized and precise on this very tall and heavy purpose-built trolley and he was going into my section with that month's stationary order. I looked at the trolley and the lift door opened at the same time. The invitation was too tempting. I pushed the trolley into the lift, pressed the button in the lift and traveled up to the top floor. This floor was vacant and did not belong to CICB. Once there, I pushed out the trolley as far as I could, found a deserted corner and left it there. I then returned to the 5th floor. Spence was still was nowhere to be seen. I then walked into my section, sat at my desk as if nothing had happened. Spencer was talking to a fellow colleague about something and I pretended I was doing my work. I never found out when he found his trolley, or if he ever did. He never mentioned it to me, or anyone else, about it disappearing into thin air.

Another distraction which helped me tolerate the boredom of the job was that U started talking and questioning me as to why she had not become pregnant yet. Obviously, I had my suspicions. It was not as if I was trying to avoid it. I only knew that my agenda was that every time we had sex, I was hoping that it would happen naturally and she would conceive. It did not happen. U asked me to take her to the doctor, to be checked out. I told her to leave it to me and I would get checked out first. At the time I was not sure if she would have suspected anything wrong, or that she may have assumed that I knew something was not right with me. She agreed easily. Maybe she was too much of a lady to ask any questions. Well, I went to see my regular consultant who authorized me to have a few tests and fertility treatment was soon prescribed.

In those days the course of treatment that I was given was an injection once every two weeks which should cause the body to react and start producing sperm in seventy-two days. I could never understand how it all came about in seventy-two days or if was that an average. Well, those seventy-two days were the longest I had ever waited. I booked an appointment for a test and a sperm count at the end of this time. Miraculously and unbelievably the test proved positive and I was producing sperm. Sex was now planned every five days and again miraculously U became pregnant. I personally and internally was ecstatic! I had raised my emotions so high I was walking with a smile on my face 24/7. But I was brought down to earth as quickly as I had been lifted up. U felt a pain in her side, started to bleed and miscarried. I felt that I was more upset than her, I cried for days, I felt guilty, I thought it was my fault, it may have been the treatment, I questioned everything. My consultant told me it could have been anything, it may have been nature's way, as the baby may have had a flaw, or that U may have overstretched herself. This apparently was common. Going to work had become difficult and I had problems coping mentally. I often found myself crying at my desk, and I spent more time in my hideaway on my own, feeling sorry for myself.

I had not stopped having the treatment at the time as my doctor had told me there was a good possibility that U would get pregnant again as after miscarriage women are more fertile and getting pregnant was easier. U just blamed her miscarriage on 'evil eyes and past curses' as well as the neighbour's jealousy of her happiness. I was happy with her way of thinking, it suited me.

About three months after U had her miscarriage she discovered that she was pregnant again. Well this time, as far as I was concerned U was going to be wrapped in cotton wool. I wanted this baby more than anything. The next nine months were endless. At work a memorandum was circulated about a fast track promotion scheme. I satisfied the criteria and applied to become an Administration Officer. I was over qualified for what I was doing and was promoted. The only problem was that word had got around that 'I did not take my job seriously' – which was Pete being politically correct! I could not stay in the department I was in. However I was always interested in immigration matters. The Immigration and Nationality Department was very busy and needed staff so it was what you call a natural progression. I was soon posted to Croydon's Immigration department. Once again other matters were on my mind and work was the last thing on my mind. U was now in her last days of her pregnancy. I could not wait.

Gemma was born in late 1988. I was present at the birth and remember the baby being born. She was placed in a plastic see-though bowl-type crib. The nurse delicately laid Gemma on her back and wrapped her like an egg. I remember her looking up at me, with the biggest black eyes I had ever seen. I remember looking at her and saying to her that I loved her like nothing I had ever loved before. I would look after and care for her as long as I lived.

Before I got settled in my new post in Croydon I heard from my old colleagues at CICB   that Pete had reached his peak at CICB and for him to progress he needed to change departments, so he soon followed me to IND. We were not in the same section, but we soon linked up and our relationship as work colleagues changed and we became friends.

Traveling daily from north London to Croydon was very time consuming, tiring and was making me ill. The building I was based inside in East Croydon was in an open area. This was very windy and cold and when I used to walk from the train station to the Headquarters of the IND I used to get chest pains and thought I was going to have a heart attack. This daily routine was very unpleasant and I sought a transfer. Now that I was a father, money became more important in life. I was now beginning to accept being in a loveless marriage but did like being a daddy. I needed to put my thinking hat on and now start making money. The house that we had bought was paying for itself, so that was a good start. Well, it should have been. I found myself with more money than I ever did before, and now gambled more. I found myself gambling bigger stakes; I would go into the betting shop, for a few minutes, but end up being in there all day. There was a betting shop immediately outside Croydon railway Station, which did not help. I would go in and have a bet after work, almost every evening. The only times I did not go in was when I did not have any money. I remember one day, I was supposed to start work at 11am, so I took my time to go to work and arrived at Croydon station about 10.30am. I had time to waste. It was payday that day, so I checked my balance in the local bank's ATM and yes I'd got paid. I think I had about £600 pounds in it. I withdrew £10 and thought to myself I would pop into the betting shop to have a bet on the morning greyhound racing. Well, the usual happened. I lost. I then bet on the second race and lost that one too. By this time I would have been late for work. My focus, then changed. I needed to get my money back, so what was I going to do? I knew it was 'chasing' but I was a gambler and this was how it worked. I withdrew some more money and carried on losing, then went backward and forwards from the ATM to the betting shop. I was forced to stop when the ATM told me I had reached my limit. I then went into the bank and withdrew money over the counter. Nothing was going to stop me. I was going to get my money back. The more money I lost the bigger risk I had to take. Eventually, I lost all that month's salary.

Whilst gambling, I was in a daze, I did not think of the consequences, I did not remember I had a child or a wife, I did not think how was I going to survive the coming month, how I was going to pay for my travel to work. I was no longer in the mood to do anything, I was supposed to be at work, I had lost over £600 in less than two hours in the betting shop and work was waiting for me. What was I doing? I kept on saying to myself 'I WAS NO FUCKING GOOD. I WAS NO FUCKING GOOD!' It was not the first time I would swear to myself, call myself a mug and wish I could put a bullet into my head. I decided to go back home, so I phoned work from a telephone box and made an excuse as to why I was not coming in that day and took the next train back to London. On the train, I was thinking, how I was going to cover up my actions without anyone knowing. How was I going to balance this month's expenses? I decided not to pay the mortgage that month and use the rental income to cover for my mistakes. Before I knew it I would miss other months of mortgage payments and soon was in a lot of payment arrears.

A New Idea

Interestingly, fortunately, or coincidently, depending on how I wanted to see it, during this period Pete was posted to the Asylum Section dealing with Asylum seekers from Cyprus and Turkey. He came up with the idea that we should start an immigration company, giving information and help in extending visas to stay in the UK. We talked about this idea often but I never took it seriously or thought that it was viable. Whilst visiting relatives I went into a little sweet shop, next door to my auntie's fish bar in Tonbridge Kent, which I thought could be a good video films rental business. I talked to the old man serving me at the time, who I later learned was Mr. Shaw, the owner. Off the cuff, I mentioned to him that if he ever wanted to sell his shop, he should contact me. I never thought he would but I left him my contact details. Mr. Shaw told me that he was not ready to retire or thinking of it so I did not raise any hopes. The shop felt and looked as if it belonged to another time zone. It reminded me of shops of the 1960's – it did have a warm feeling about it. It was as if it was my destiny because he rang my home number on the following Monday to say that he was interested in selling. I then told Pete of my idea of the video business and that I would be leaving the Home Office. He laughed and told me that I was wasting my time. We discussed that in the event of things not working out, we should work on setting up an Immigration Advisory service. We both agreed to re-evaluate the situation in a year's time. I'm sure both of us at that time did not foresee how the future was going to unfold.

Buying Mr. Shaw's shop was a blessing for me. I now needed to find finance to buy the shop, so I decided to sell the house in London and buy a new home for my family nearer to the shop. I could now pay off the mortgage arrears that I had built up because of my gambling, as I had the chance to make more money than I could ever working for the Home Office. Most importantly, I thought it was a chance for me and U to start again and try and build on a relationship that may include some sort of love.

My little family unit moved and settled in Tonbridge. This move was meant to be the start of U and my new life together. We had bought our own home. I had set up a small business. We had a lovely but spoilt baby, we were on our own now living away from the family who could not interfere with anything in anyway but this in reality, was the real beginning of the end. Obviously I did not know this at the time but instead of U and I getting closer and building on what we had set up, we slowly but surely started to grow apart. I soon realized and accepted I was on my own in this marriage and that U was more of an individual, egotistical and extremely self-interested. By this time I started not liking U anymore and day to day the strings holding our marriage together were snapping one by one. So what did I decide that I needed to do? I decided to have another child. Logic was also not my thing! I knew it was time that I had a son. I put the idea it in my head and it soon became a compulsion. I now wanted that son. Well, I decided it was time, told U and she did not mind as she always wanted another child. Naci wanted it to happen so it will happen. I was on another personal mission, obsessed.

Firstly I had to convince my doctor to re-start the fertility treatment. I knew U could not conceive if I did not have the treatment.

As usual, when I was in that frame of mind nothing was going to stop me. I easily convinced my GP that my family needed another child to be complete and he agreed to the treatment and funding was authorized. U got pregnant soon after the seventy-two day period and from the minute that she told me she was pregnant I knew it was a boy, a son. I planned around the boy being born, called the fetus a 'he' and was buzzing, looking forward to him being born. I would talk to customers who visited my shop about the baby, referring to it as my son.

One day whilst working in the shop, a female customer walked in, hair wet through. I looked at her and then through the shop window but it was not raining outside. I remember asking her if it had been raining. She said no, it was not, she told me that she had just come out of the bath. I laughed and said, ok. I looked at her; she was obviously a blonde and had the most powerful seductive blue eyes, such that I had never seen - maybe it was the bath water, but her eyes were just gorgeous. I smiled and just looked, keeping my thoughts to myself. She had the confidence of a local, but I had never seen her before. Who was she?

I found out that this was Sarah. She had just recently moved to the house down the road from my shop and every time she came to my shop she left with a bit of my heart. I was falling in love with her fast. I loved her look, indeed, everything about her. She quickly became a regular customer who would come in for long chats. We spoke for hours. She would take her children to school and pop in to the shop before going back home. At the time I do not think she knew how much I had fallen for her, but I am sure she knew that I fancied her. I could not have made it more obvious. Sarah opened my eyes and it was confirmed to me she was the most perfect women in my world, 'the blonde with blue eyes'. U was now nine months pregnant and I was looking forward to the birth of my son.

It was Saturday and I was in the shop with my dad, preparing for that day's trade when U rang to tell me that her waters had broken and she felt that the baby was coming. I rushed home and took her to hospital. Three hours later after a comfortable labour U had the baby. It was a girl! I could not believe it, I had raised hope within myself and believed that it was going to be a boy. I was truly, fully and unashamedly very upset. I walked out of the delivery room and outside of the hospital to get some fresh air. I just burst out in tears and passers-by must have thought I had heard bad news. I was just disappointed, and realised it was no-one's fault but my own. I was transfixed with the idea of having a boy and I was wrong.

We named her Honey, which was U's oldest sister's name.

After Honey was born Sarah fever was taking over and growing more and more in my heart. Sarah was the only reason I looked forward to and could not wait to open the shop in the morning. Waiting for her visits and chats were the best thing of the day. The business was dying a small death, the demand for video films were declining, 'Sky' had come on the scene and people all around the estate were installing free satellite dishes. They could now watch movies without leaving their homes. Then one day the phone rang. It was Pete.

We spoke about things, the situation of economy and the state of the business. He told me that he had now established himself well enough and that I should look into setting up the immigration company. I should start off by offering clients the chance to stay in the UK indefinitely. The decision was not difficult to make as the idea of establishing and building up the company ticked all the right boxes for me. The idea excited me, in that it would make me money. The business of renting out videos was finished so I needed another income. However, overall it was the thrill and buzz factor of doing something illegal that thrilled me the most. Once again going against the norm, anarchy my revenge against society, my revenge for being born the way I was. After all, I was a risk taker, a big gambler, what could happen to me? The worst thing was I would go to prison. So what! Incarceration did not scare me at the time. I thought to myself, I may even like it. I knew I would find a way to deal with the situation if it happened. So whilst running a failing business in Tonbridge that was struggling to survive, I put a very small five line advert in a popular Turkish Newspaper. I remember, wording it as; Ex Home Office Worker, Immigration Advisor, Visa Extensions - ring this number. It was that easy.

My dad would come down from London on week-ends to give me some respite from the shop and on Wednesdays I would arrange to see clients who had immigration problems either in London or at my home. I was slowly creating a small business which would help support me and my family financially. Potential clients would ring me, and I would discuss their immigration situation with them. Listening to these vulnerable and anxious people made me realize that I was sitting on a gold mine. I could charge and make whatever money I wanted as long as Pete could deliver. I was often given whatever I asked for in a financial deposit, offered bonuses if I could do what I said I would do. I was sometimes threatened by others who told me that I would be shot if I did not. The intimidation and fear factor did not bother me in the least, not because I was this courageous brave man, but I think I was naive in a way and embraced the power given to me. I now had all these people asking me for help and I now knew that I was seen differently - I was now recognized as A 'somebody!' I felt that finally, I had the supremacy to 'screw' a British government department by beating them and their system and getting revenge for the feelings of disrespect they had shown me from day one. Then there was the bonus of the money that I could make. I loved it.

Moving to Kent was not the dream move that I was hoping for. I thought that opening a video shop in this location would have been successful. I did not anticipate the problems that came with the move. The scariest aspect was that of not being accepted. A small minority of the community thought I was an Asian and I was called the P word on many occasions by locals who lived around the vicinity of the shop. Name-calling was not the worst form of racism; the shop window was broken on more than four occasions, always on a Saturday night soon after I had closed up and was driving home. I would pull up outside my home which was five minutes away from the shop. The phone would ring and the security company that protected the property would inform me that the alarms of the shop had been triggered and activated. It was not difficult to find out who was smashing the window over and over again, on the same day, at the same time, of every week. The matter had become an issue of local gossip and the talking point of the estate.

I was informed by more than one customer, who the culprit was, namely a David Roberts. Ironically he was a member of the video club, part of a very big well-known and respected family in the area. Everybody knew where he lived and interestingly his family members were good and generous customers. It was alleged that Roberts was an ex-soldier who had recently returned back from fighting in the Falklands war and could not cope with living outside the army life and he had developed a vendetta against anyone who was not British. No one would admit to seeing him do it, or corporate with police inquiries. Even the Police did not know how to deal with the situation. The smashing of the window stopped when I was forced to put up shutters by the insurance company that covered the business. This though did not stop the racist attacks.

It was about 9.45pm on a Saturday night and I was in the back stock room, whilst my father was in the front of the shop. I heard a big bang and then rushed to the front. My dad looked pale and I could see the fear in his face. I looked over to the direction where he was looking, and saw a display shelf had been forcibly been broken off its brackets and all the stock was on the floor. I remember my dad saying to me, "Son, it's time for you to get your family together and leave, that soldier done this, he came in and told me that he was going to burn the shop down and kill all of us". I was worried more for my dad at that present time, than Roberts' threats. It was at that time that I consciously made the decision it was the right time to move. I knew of a local man who wanted to buy the business and contacted him. We quickly agreed a price, and completed the sale within the month. The video business was now sold. Contracts had been agreed and signed to lease out our home to the local council who would then rent out the house to a homeless family. Removal Lorries were packed and after three years we were all returning back to London, back where we started. The house was in negative equity and the rent agreed with the council was not enough to cover the mortgage. But because of the awful time we had experienced in Tonbridge, moving back to London at the time was the right decision. The only positive thing that came out of my life in Tonbridge was the addition of another child to my family.

My relationship with Sarah was escalating. I told her that I would leave my wife and that I was not happy in my marriage but she insisted that she did not want to be a part of my marriage breaking up or me divorcing my wife. We went out on a few dates but she was adamant that she was not going to encourage me to leave my wife. I told her that I would divorce U, with or without her. She did not believe me when I left Tonbridge. I left with that question once again that's always lingering in my head, once again - What if?

When I came back to London from Tonbridge I needed to reinvest the little money I had come out with from the sale of the shop. I knew my weaknesses. I did not want to gamble it away. I knew as long as the money was accessible I would dip into the funds to gamble. I would lose then chase my 'losses' by taking riskier bets, eventually losing the lot. I put the money towards a down payment and took out a mortgage and bought a freehold building that was suitable for bed-sit letting. It also had a shop which was let as a greengrocers shop. I soon started earning a good living from rental income, as property prices were raising quickly in London and my investment was paying off. Whenever I went to collect the rent, I would visit a café next door to my building. I started to talk to the owner, who wanted to sell it. I took out another bank loan on the equity on my freehold building to finance the purchase of the café. I bought it and started to run the café with my mother and father. I was now running a café from 6.30am in the morning, till 7pm in the evening. I felt that I had reached my pinnacle, running a café as well as being a landlord renting out properties. Making money was now not an issue, it was looking after it.

The café was very busy and was taking more of my time that I wanted to give it. I was now making money from all my businesses; rental income from my property, the Immigration Company and now the café. But as fast as I was making money, I spent it. I paid my parents for their labours in the café and I made sure we all continued as a family to go on holiday every year. My father did love his annual treat to Florida. If there was any money left, I gambled it in the betting shops. I did not worry about spending money or what I lost gambling because I knew property prices were getting higher and my expensive hobby was being paid for. As property prices were going up, I was borrowing on the equity again and again. I used to put a little deposit down and buy another property to let out. At the time I thought it was an easy way to make money and thought that my luck would never end. Before I knew it I had three other freehold properties that I was renting out.

I was now truly back and settling back in London and my immigration advice business was now growing. Word of mouth was spreading within my circle of associates on how I was now making a reputation for myself. Many people were inquiring on how I could help them or they knew someone with an immigration matter who would benefit from my sources. At the same time, I was also involved in a 'Beer Run', back and forth to France. Once or twice weekly I went with my brother-in-law Ali, who was married to U's youngest sister. He and I would drive to Dover, hop on a ferry to Calais and bring back cheap beer that was sent from the UK in the first place, now duty free and sell them on to off-licenses. Ali and I were of the same age and had similar interests. We even looked like each other. A lot of people thought we were brothers. The fact that we were both married to sisters meant that we spent a lot of time together. Apart from distributing the beers, we socialized together as a family. Ali had an elder sister, H. This was how I first saw, met and got to know H.

H

H was always in the background as Ali lived a few houses away from his mother and H spent a lot of time at her mother's. She was very friendly and chatty. She had just recently started divorce proceedings with the husband of her three children. This made talking to her easier, in that she was not someone's wife. She would often discuss friends she knew who needed my immigration advice. Together we arranged to help these friends with their problems and H would get a commission from my fees. The arrangement suited everyone and this is how we basically became friends. H had a little gold-coloured car and would drive me to see her friends. We started becoming closer friends. I told her about my past. I told her about Sarah, she told me about her past and how unhappy she was because of her marriage failing. At this time I did not think for one minute that any romance would have blossomed and five years into the future I would be marrying her. H was a plump, very voluptuous woman. She had those beautiful, talking eyes, blue eyes that just said "make love to me" that was my weakness. I thought Sarah had the best eyes I had ever seen, but H could have easily been selected to advertise designer glasses. Her eyes were what attracted me to her at first and even talking to her was embarrassing for me as face to face those eyes were just too provocative. It was such a new experience for me. I liked her, but the difference this time was that I knew that she was falling for me too. Was it because she was vulnerable after her marriage ending? I just thrived on the new attention from this beautiful woman. She told me she liked the rough side of me and the way I carried out my business affairs. Naturally I loved all of it! My marriage had reached its peak, it would have never got better and I felt that U and I were drifting apart. We had started disrespecting each other which I thought was a sign of the end. I started noticing and disliking U's wicked and cruel side, as well how self-centered she was. This made the distraction of spending time with another woman a lot easier for me. I felt no guilt as I saw this as the end and not a fling. My marriage was over, only question was, when?

Ali would describe H as his 'mad' sister. Mad was his definition of her and I esteemed her madness and unpredictability. I always did and always will. I often smile to myself when I think about her ways and behaviour at first. Maybe this is what made me fall in love with her so soon. She was another rebel. On this particular Monday Ali and I had returned from France after doing our usual beer run the night before and returned back home. I bought a bottle of Chanel Chance perfume for H from the Duty Free shop and gave Ali the gift to give to his sister. This was going to be a busy day. Later in the day I was going to represent a client who had an appointment to be interviewed by the Immigration Department in Croydon about a visa problem. Whilst waiting in the Immigration and Nationality waiting area, my mobile phone rang and it was H. She thanked me for the gift and then pleasantly shocked me: telling me that she "loved me". I remember punching the air as if I had won something. This was the first time another woman had genuinely told me that she was in love with me. I was shaken but at the same time so happy. It did not matter at that time that I was married, a father, or the fact that H was my brother- in-law's sister. All these consequences were irrelevant. A woman was in love with me and I had craved for this all my life. It did not take much for me to know what I wanted. I needed to be loved by someone and I did not care about anything or anyone else.

H soon became besotted and sometimes neurotic towards me, which I found very scary at times but I thrived on these feelings, without letting H know. I was head over heels in love also. Well eventually, and without any planning, H and I physically committed ourselves to our relationship and to each other. To me this was a new experience. I wanted it to be special and serious, as this was going to be a very significant and poignant move in my life. I knew after this my marriage to U was definitely over. Before the act of love, I asked H if she was sure this is what she wanted and that for me there would be no going back. She just nodded her head. We both wanted it. The day was a day to remember. It was also H's mother's birthday.

My relationship with H had now begun, we were a couple. To H it was more her and me, to me it was both of us, plus my family. I loved this feeling of being loved by someone, who wanted me for me. H started to dye her hair blonde and with those seductive blue eyes, became a 'trophy' on my arm. I do not know how much H knew but she was good for me, she boosted my ego, made me feel greater than I ever had before. She had a tattoo done on her shoulder because I thought it was sexy. I started to love H's eccentric oppressiveness more and more, never tiring of it. Although at times her complex behavior was getting in the way of my business life, I found ways to cope with it. She would telephone me constantly, so frequently that I had to switch off my mobile phone and then she would telephone my landline at the café. Her behaviour to anyone else would have been viewed as scary and creepy but I thrived on and loved the attention she was giving me. She would be very protective over me and would even fight members of the public It did not matter where we were, in a supermarket, in a pub or in the street. If she ever overheard anyone making any comments about my size she did not hesitate to retaliate. I remember once we were both sitting in a restaurant in China Town when she heard two young men sitting by a table next to ours saying something about me. Without any hesitation or warning she turned around and embarrassed them, by saying something to them. It all happened too fast for me to realize what actually did occur, all I remember H saying was, that "she had sorted it".

Having a 'mistress' meant there were not enough hours in the day to spread myself out. I did not know it at the time, but I had taken on too much too quickly. As well as the businesses, I wanted to have an affair with another woman! Days would pass when I had not slept, at all because of the demands on my time. After work, I would go to H's house, sometimes well after midnight, spend the night with her, then go on to and open the café early in the morning, then distribute the beers I had bought back from France, followed by interview potential customers who had immigration issues. The demon of gambling had not gone away, and I would find time to gamble whenever I could. I gambled on the fruit machines, on the ferries, going to and coming from France, often losing more money in them than I would make by selling the beers. I often gambled the café takings in the betting shop next door. It did not matter as the immigration business was prosperous, so I could cover my losses without anyone else knowing.

Pete the Inside Man

I was now getting a reputation within the Turkish and Kurdish community. Word of mouth had spread that I genuinely had an 'insider' working in the immigration service who could deliver promises. Pete always told me that I was not charging clients enough and my fees were too low. He knew of other agencies and solicitor firms who charged higher fees, for far less work. He also told me to spread the word that we had the capabilities and a scheme that would guarantee clients a visa to stay in the United Kingdom, indefinitely. This, though, would be very expensive. The idea was that clients who had exhausted all the channels and ways to stay in the country and were now waiting in the queue to be deported, would benefit in two ways. Firstly, for a fee, Pete would remove a client's file from the waiting queue. Giving it to me, I would show the client the file then destroy it in front of them. This would then mean that the client could never be deported. Secondly, we would let some time pass and approach the Home Office and ask what was happening in our clients' case, asking when the client would be deported. The Home Office would not be able to find the client's files or any notes and then reluctantly and embarrassingly admit to the client they had mislaid the file. They would then grant the client a visa to stay in the country on humanitarian grounds.

The plan was very well thought out by Pete and once I had showed the client his file, it was not difficult to convince them to part with their money. What Pete did not anticipate was that fraud officers were investigating other scams within the Home Office Immigration Department involving some illegal stamping of visa stamps in passports. The police heard Pete talking to me on the telephone when I was in my mother's house about a potential 'clean up' and a 'car valet' which was a simple code to say that a file needed to be taken and a client's history needed to be cleaned up. It really did not take an Enigma code breaker to understand our code. It did not take long for the Police Fraud squad to arrest us both.

I had just arrived in London after a long drive from Calais, after doing a beer run early that morning. I had parked the van up, and still living with U in the same house, was getting ready to get some sleep, before going on to work in the café. I had not slept the night before after driving all night. My phone rang. Iit was my mother. She sounded scared and panicky, telling me that her house had been raided by the police and asking where I was. I rushed over to the house and was greeted by four tall, very angry, intimidating Police Officers, who told me that they were arresting me for illegally stamping passports. My immediate reaction to that accusation was, "No mate, I 'aint accepting that, if that's what you think, you have got it wrong." The police officer then advised me that my partner Pete had been arrested also and that they would like to go to my house as it was obvious that they were at the wrong address. I quickly knew, as they would say, "a fair cop" and I immediately made my mind up to cooperate, knowing that I was guilty as hell, so why go through a lengthy interrogation. But for a minute, I did think about it… how I could complicate matters by making it hard for the authorities? I suppose the timing of the day played a part; I was too tired to play games. I also knew that once I had gone home they would find a client's file anyway in one of my drawers. Leaving my mother's house and being escorted in handcuffs gave me a buzz, in a sick way. I did not feel any sense of shame. On the contrary, I was hoping the neighbors could see me although I imagine my mother was very scared and ashamed.

When we arrived at my home, I lead the police to my so-called office. It was all very civil and I tried to be as polite as possible, thinking at the same time in my mind what strategies to use. I remember offering tea or coffee to them and asking U if she could make the drinks. I spoke to her in Turkish and one of the officers told me not to speak in my 'lingo'. I laughed and replied back to him, if I don't speak in my own lingo, you won't get the coffee you want. I instantly knew that was the police officer that I liked the least. He commented, in a patronizing way, take this serious son, you're in trouble. Without knowing it at the time I unconsciously went into my child mode and from then on did not behave maturely, or seriously.

The police then started to put procedures in place. I just lay on the spare single bed in the room and watched how serious the police were doing their jobs, again thinking to myself and laughing inside. They were putting everything possible into see-through plastic evidence bags, literally everything. Bank books, savings books, leaflets, posters, and then they found the client's file and they thought they had found the evidence needed. One of the police officers shouting out Bingo! He then asked me where I got it from. I quickly answered "you know where I got it". The police then all consensually agreed to take my computer as evidence. I thought to myself, these people think they have solved the crime of the century and I was the Godfather! They phoned for extra vehicles to take the evidence they had gathered up. They even demanded to take an old metal office filing cabinet for forensics. I was happy to get rid of it so I literally played along with them. It was now time to go to the police station and the vehicles had arrived to take me away and all the evidence that they thought would be useful. They took everything that was in the room apart from the single bed. By that time I was getting tired, I still had not had any sleep. I was taken from my home to a waiting police van in handcuffs. I remember being pushed into the van like I was scum, then the van rushing off as fast as possible, just like a scene from a film. Looking through the van window I noticed that I was entering Edmonton Police Station, through the back entrance. Once in the station and confronted with serious and stern faces looking at me, to be honest, it was the first time that I did start to get slightly worried. After checking me in, I was led to a cell.

The cell looked very clean and smelt of disinfectant and bleach. It looked rather comfortable too. It had its own chrome toilet in it, a waterproof mattress and white tiled walls, floor to ceiling, looking like a vet's clinic. I was told that I was going to be locked in and would be interviewed in the next couple of hours. I started to panic a little when I was told about being locked up, claustrophobia was kicking in. I needed to sleep so my fears were quickly quashed. I asked for a blanket because it was a bit cold. The custody sergeant laughed out loud and told me that I was not in the Savoy Hotel. I sat on the stone hard bed, heard the lock of the door click and just thought to myself, now I was alone, really alone. I laid myself down, looking at the ceiling and walls. I started counting the wall tiles, one by one. Before long I was asleep.

I really don't know how long I was asleep, but it was a deep sleep, I was awoken by another duty officer, and told that I was needed to be interviewed. I asked if I had any choice, because I would have preferred to sleep. In a stern voice, the policeman told me that I did not have any choice. I was led to a small room and greeted by two of my arresting police officers. When I entered the room I was asked to sit down, told I was going to be interviewed and that the interview would be tape recorded and a video made. I then started stroking my hair, pretending I was making myself look beautiful. I then asked the policeman which one was going to be 'good cop, and who was going to play bad?' One of them replied to my question by saying I had been watching too much television. I then asked them if I could have a cigarette, although I did not smoke, but I thought I wanted to enjoy every moment of this. It really was a surreal moment for me. The questions started to flow and I answered them as truthfully and honestly as I knew how. I soon lost any fear I had of the situation and quickly started to like both interviewing police officers and became relaxed. Maybe the police were well trained and intentionally played their police roles well. I was offered a duty solicitor if I so desired one. I wanted this over and done with as quickly as possible. I needed to distribute the beers I had just brought over from France. I had to go and help in the cafe and I knew H would be worried as there was no way she would have heard what had happened. It did not matter to me, because I knew I was guilty as one could be. From that moment I felt I would be fighting a losing cause if I tried to defend it. I also did not have any confidence in some rookie duty solicitor. I wanted to do it my way as usual. I quickly planned my strategy and I thought to myself that I did not want anyone to know the extent of how many Home Office files I had destroyed. I did not even know myself or how much money I had made from the scam. I also was for once grateful for my gambling habit, as I had definitely squandered a lot of the money I had made from this immigration business. Consequences had worked out in my favour. I had nothing to show for my crimes. Everything I owned was mortgaged to the maximum and at the time I really did not take it seriously, once again I was being myself.

My experience of being interrogated was over quicker than I thought and the worst part was that I had to make my own way back home from the police station. I had no money, or resources to phone for a lift. I knew my dad would be running the cafe, my mum would have been worried and H would have been wondering where I had disappeared to as it had been over ten hours that we had not spoken and had not made any contact with each other. She would have sensed something was wrong. This was a very long time, as we practically spoke to each other every hour. U never even entered into my thoughts. I don't really know how U felt or thought, she was not the easiest person to understand, emotionally anyway. As soon as I could, I went home, got my car and drove to the cafe, where both my parents were by now. The first thing my father told me was that my friend H kept on ringing the café and he asked me if she was okay in the head. He asked me if I was having an affair with her. She had apparently driven him crazy, continually phoning the cafe, asking where I was and he said that he had no choice to tell her that I was in trouble. I understood the situation, I knew and had experienced H's obsessive behaviors. I was loving all this attention from her but could not tell others. They would have thought it as a sign of madness. My parents did not until then, know how close H and I had become. I phoned H and told her basically what had happened. Iit was the first time that prison was mentioned and H asked me if I was going to prison. I never thought of any custodial sentence before that. I tried to assure her that I was not though I did not know the answer to that myself. I was soon told that there would be further investigations and more interviews. I was told that I had to report to the Serious Fraud squads head office, every six weeks without any restrictions. I was surprised that I was allowed to travel abroad and my passport was not retained. Pete, apparently kept, his mouth shut and the CPS thought that there was insignificant evidence whereby he could be prosecuted, so as far as I understood it. He got away with it. I have never spoken to him since. Once again I was alone, them against me. I signed on at the Police Station for approximately five years.

I had by then built a relationship with two of the original police officers who arrested me, one of them had moved on to another department, the other one retired. Whenever I signed, on as I put it, I would be greeted by either one of the two remaining officers and we would discuss the case. I felt that both officers were quite nice people, who just thought of me as someone stupid, a likable rogue, a rough diamond, rather than a criminal. I felt I had at last made a mark and did not see the future consequences but only my 'five minutes of fame'.

In the five years before the court case, whilst the police were investigating, they allowed me to carry on with my life, although I needed to sign on every six weeks. At the time I did not know my hearing would be heard five years later. That year was no different from the previous ten years. We were, as usual, going to Florida for the Christmas festivities. The difference this year was we were going as a big group - my mum, dad, sister, U, my girls and me. Plus three other families, two of which were from my mother's side of the family. Ali and U's sister were the other. We rented two villas next door to each other. H knew of the booked holiday, obviously, as Ali was, after all, her brother and she insisted I should not go. I told her that she was being impracticable. It was too early to bring our relationship to others' attention. We compromised when I promised her I would not sleep with U whilst I was there and when I returned back to the UK, I would tell the family that I will start divorce proceedings and will be getting married to H. There were about twenty of us who went to Florida that year. It was always in my mind that that year could be my last. I spent most of the time I was there on my own, dazed and thinking about H in England.

U and her sister were obviously going to stay in one villa, so the split was easy. My family and cousins stayed in one, U, I and the kids stayed in the other with her sister, the kids and Ali. It was obvious that there was friction between U and me. Basically I did my own thing, as usual, being the clown of the group, the entertainer. U surprisingly, did not let my behaviour ruin anything and if she was worried she did well to hide it. The other house did not know that I was not sharing a bed with U. Over the ten days we were in Orange County, friction between U and I got more obvious and at times got loud, more me than her. An incident occurred in a restaurant when we were trying to arrange seating. U refused to sit next to me and at the time I did not like it. Without thinking, I blurted out to the group as if I was making a formal announcement that when I return to England I will be divorcing U. U did not say a word. She just stayed placid, showing no emotion. On reflection my behavior was irrational and rather intimidating but I did it and after so many years of marriage, think it was not the right way to do it.

When we returned to the UK I went back to my mother's house. My marriage was over. My life was now in the hands of solicitors. It did not take long to get divorced, neither of us contested it. I just wanted it over and done with. H though, wanted it more than anything and anyone. She was always pestering me, asking questions on when the divorce was going to come. Well, it did come. Financial matters needed to be sorted out. The divorce became a bitter, twisted game, for both of us. I did not anticipate U's scornful side and underestimated her intelligence and astuteness. She was hurt and wanted to hurt me. I tried to anticipative U's next move before she went to seek legal advice. I asked her not to waste money on solicitors. I proposed that I eventually would transfer all the properties that I owned to our two daughters and in the meantime, I would give her a healthy allowance every month. She adamantly refused to listen to any of my offers. She, in fact, said that she would be ruining me, pushing to bankrupt me, hoping to see me begging in the street and she would think about throwing me a coin so I could buy myself a hot drink

I think after so many years, I must be the most hated person she knows. I suppose one must expect that in a divorce. Well, the assets were split, by the courts, all the mortgaged properties were sold and any profits were put in a central kitty as the courts called it. I kept the cafe business, as it was my main income and my official job. After everything was distributed, sold and taken away, by the time U and the solicitors got their share, my inheritance, my earnings, from all the work and risks I had taken, were now gone. U definitely got the better deal. I honestly tried to give her as little as I could, but the courts did not allow it. In the end, I did not have the energy, wickedness and spitefulness in me that U had inside her, to fight on. After all, it was my entire fault.

H and I started to get to know each other better. H's eccentricities, possessiveness, obsessions, her personalities were now coming out and I loved them all. She made me laugh, she kept me on edge, but most importantly I thrived on her love for me. No one will ever know how her love for me was. She made me feel that I was a human being, a man, a person, no longer that invisible man on the outside. I did not care about her madness, her selfishness, or her nagging. She was good for me.

During those five years of waiting for the courts to decide my fate my life became rather dormant. Obviously I had stopped the beer runs, did no more immigration work and I relied on the café and income from my rental businesses. U and I stopped communicating. H was now my partner in life. U took the separation as expected very badly and continued to make my life hard as she could. U knew there was someone else but did not know who for certain, but I believe she had some idea. After all the other woman was someone that she knew- it was her sister's sister-in-law, my brother-in-law's sister. This certainly would have put a cat amongst the pigeons.

Charged

When it was time for me to be charged, I then thought it was time to employ a solicitor who came with me to Holborn's police station where I was formally charged. My solicitor then appointed barristers to defend me.

At first, I felt that the barrister firm employed by my solicitor was not very good, after various meetings with them and my barrister who was a young Chinese girl, called Su Li. I was not very confident with the senior partners and less confident with Su Li, as I felt she was inexperienced. I was guilty and everyone around me knew I was going to be given a custodial sentence. It was just how long? I was told that I could be given up to ten years. I knew deep down that I would never go to prison that long. I thought to myself I needed to find a strategy and put it in place in case things were really going against me. I thought of the idea of maybe trying to persuade the courts that I had mental health issues, so I arranged with my GP's help to get some counseling. At the time, I was playing the mental health tag, but once I started my first ever counseling, I realized that I truly did have some personal issues that needed to be explored. My first six counseling sessions told me the obvious, that I was a spoilt man who never grew up, I needed to be more serious and that I should stop thinking that I was the family's prince. I needed to start taking responsibility. During the counseling sessions, we discussed my gambling addiction and my escapism in gambling which was an example of me not taking any responsibility. My gambling addiction and my compulsive eating ran parallel. The counselor pointed out throughout my life my eating disorder had led me to take drastic actions to satisfy this dependence that I had on food. I stole food, I deceived to buy food but I had not been desperate enough to steal money to gamble.

Unfortunately and sadly, Su li was involved in a very infamous train crash in Potters Bar and was killed which meant the barrister firm needed to appoint another barrister to take on my case. Arthur Crowley, QC, came out of retirement and was very interested in my case. He was a very experienced barrister, who specialized in fraud cases. After all these years, my final day had come and I was going to be tried at Southwark Crown Court. My barrister advised me to plead not guilty and I took on his advice, which was against my opinion. I thought pleading guilty would be a quicker solution and if there was any chance of me going to prison, I would go for less time. My barrister was a very charismatic, 70-year-old; I respected and loved his brains, I believed in him and felt that he cared for his clients. So I took on his advice and at first pleaded not guilty. Juries were selected and I had a Sikh judge. I was asked if I was happy with the jury. From where I was sitting I could not see any members of the black and ethnic community and I questioned this matter with my barrister, not because I really cared, I just wanted to be petty, and rebellious. Mr. Crowley laughed at my comment and told me to look at the judge. I just grinned and nodded.

I went to court every day, with my sister, two of my cousins who commuted from Kent daily, my brother-in- law and one of my regular customers of the cafe that I used to spend time with, which I thought was a nice gesture, and of course, H. At this moment of time nobody apart from me and H knew how close we were. I often ask myself, did her brother have any idea what H and I had together? I remember my poor little sister's emotional state; she was not coping with the situation very well and whilst sitting in the dock I often found myself looking back to her to see how she was coping. When the court watched the recorded video of my interview, I remember my sister shaking her head at some of my antics, especially when I asked for a cigarette. I remember her commenting and saying out loud "He does not even smoke". I also remember the judge making a note, once when the policeman asked me in the interview, did I know what I was doing, and what did I expect would happen if I got caught. The judge looked intrigued by my reply and shook his head when I said "I did not really think about what I was doing, and thought if I got caught, I thought I would just get slapped on the wrist and be let off". Often, whilst sitting in the defendant's box, I got bored of the day's proceedings and became restless. The bailiffs, seated on either side of me, often reminded me that my behavior was not appropriate and that I should try not to upset the judge, but it was not long before I would forget their advice and would try to entertain myself. On one occasion, I took a little die-cast toy car into the box with me and started to push the car around on the table I was sitting behind. The bailiffs, were shocked, I do not think they had seen anything so absurd. At the time, I do not know why I behaved in that way, maybe I was just trying to be funny and arrogant at the same time, telling the world, I did not care, or maybe I was trying to show the jury how stupid I was?

My barrister put forward his case that I had not committed any crime and technically what I was alleged to have done was not a recognized criminal offense. This was not allowed by the judge. My QC also wanted the judge to take into account the time delay and failure of the crown prosecution service in getting the case into court. The judge did not accept that the time factor was not a reason not to allow the case to be heard. After a week of evidence presented by the prosecution and negotiations, my barrister came back to me to tell me to change my plea. He told me to expect and accept that I may be going to prison for up to ten years but more than likely I would be going to prison for two years. My barrister did, however, tell me whatever sentence I would be given, I had the right of appeal and would be released in about twelve months. If the appeal was proven I would be famous and when I heard that word 'famous' I looked at him; "Yes, famous!" he said. At the time I did not understand but I knew I had no choice but to take my barrister's advice and immediately started to accept the future. So I changed my plea to a guilty one. The jury was then dismissed. The judge then looked at me: He read out to the court whilst looking at me, I just looked down, at my feet, not so much in shame but in, respect for him. I remember only two points of his summing up. Firstly the judge said that my actions had put Great Britain's security position in jeopardy, I had found a way that could allow undesirable people and organizations such as criminals and terrorists, to remain, which could have catastrophic consequences. I did this for my own financial gain. Secondly, and at the time, more importantly, which made me look up and face him, the judge looked at me and began to sum up, then told me to go away and come back in two weeks' time and when I returned, I should expect a custodial sentence.

The next day I remember my court case had made headline news in a few popular national newspapers. VISAS TO TAKE AWAY - KEBAB SHOP OWNER IN IMMIGRATION SCAM was one of the headlines, which was quite disappointing, as my business was a cafe, not a kebab shop. My barrister was right, I was famous. The following two weeks were very difficult. It was the first time that I had accepted that I was going to go to prison. Not knowing how long was the big question. I remember at the time a regular customer of my cafe, Big Dave, who came to my cafe especially, to see me and advise me. He was knowledgeable about the prison way of life and what I could expect. He just told me to keep my head down, just focus on my release date and remember that the person I was sharing my cell with will be most probably leaving prison a long time after you. He told me to have a good stock of batteries and a good radio. Prison is a lonely life, especially at the weekends, where, because of staff cutbacks, you could be locked up twenty-three hours a day. The advice was taken on board. I was more afraid of the lonely times and thought about trying to entertain myself. I had always been claustrophobic before that, but when I heard that, I would not close my bedroom door at night, whenever I went to bed. For many years afterward, I even dreamt that I would die of suffocation.

The two weeks quickly came and the hardest moment was saying bye-bye to my children the night before. I did not say bye-bye to U. She obviously hated me, and I really felt nothing for her. Honey was a bit young to understand. Gemma though, did look scared and worried. My parents did not have the emotional strength to come to court and chose to stay and run the cafe. Saying bye to them was in a way harder, my parents were worried. If I were to go to prison they would not be able to cope with the business of running the cafe. They were too old and were hoping to retire anyway. I never thought about such a problem, maybe I took advantage and overlooked that my parents could ever leave me. What would I do if I went to prison? Even worse for me was the thought that it would be impossible for me to stay at the café and run it. I could not imagine settling and staying in one place. The cafe had to be put up for sale. I was not thinking too well at that time, but life-changing decisions had to be made quickly and most of them were not the right ones. The divorce was very stressful, all of the matrimonial court cases had mentally drained me. H started to become serious, she wanted us to spend more and more time together, she would express her opinion, which was not mine. My head was very confused.

I had not been able to sell the café. Plan B was put in place. I had arranged with a friend, that if I had to serve a custodial sentence, he would take over the cafe business, run it himself and he could take all the profits but give my dad a weekly rent which he would put away for me. I would take the business back when I came out of prison. Fourteen days flew past and my destiny was soon to be revealed.

I felt shame and guilt for putting everyone in this position, especially my parents. I had let them down. My mother did not deserve this. My father would put on his rare disappointed face and assure me that God would look after me. He told me not to worry as the business would run itself. I took the train to court this time, for obvious reasons and the rest of my supporters were already waiting for me when I got there. I was going to be sentenced in the afternoon but before any sentencing, the police wanted to ask me more questions.

The police tried to offer me a deal and told me there was a chance I could get a lesser sentence if I could give them any more information. I knew at that moment they were still making further inquiries, maybe looking for more arrests, looking for more information, on Peter. On both accounts, I could not help, however much I wanted to. I was becoming scared, really afraid but I had nothing to offer. I remember my barrister advising me to leave any principles I held in the past, it was time to forget them if there was an occasion to save myself, saying "Naci if there is a time to save your own arse, now was it". I had nothing to give. Everyone in the room; police, my barrister, legal assistants, everyone seemed disappointed. We all looked at each other, the consensus of thought was, I was going to prison.

The meeting was over; I was going to meet up with my family and friends, for the last time. We were going to eat together in the court's canteen. Whilst in the restaurant I sat down and wrote everyone's address that was there, I planned to write letters to everyone. Big Dave's advice was haunting me. 2.00 o'clock quickly came by. My time had come; finally I would be punished, sentenced. Five years of ups and downs, in sixty months I had lost almost everything that I had. The immigration business was gone. I had divorced my children's mother. The cafe business was not making any money and my assets were now being ripped apart by divorce lawyers. The beer run was over. Now the Establishment was going to put me away. "Whoever said, you give a man enough rope he will hang himself" must have been thinking of me when he said it.

The jokes and clowning around, me pretending that I did not care, were now over. I walked into the defendant's box, my court bailiffs already waiting for me, one standing on each side of an empty chair. I recognized one, who smiled at me. I acknowledged her with a look of helplessness and shame. I was not familiar with the other bailiff, who was another black female. Obviously those above did not think I was going to be any trouble. Well, there was no real threat of me running away. My barrister started his summing up first. He reminded the judge and the rest of the court that I had been a good citizen for the last five years. I had kept out of trouble, had been running my own business and was now in a settled relationship, with a lady who had children. He also reminded the judge that I financially supported my own children and was not a burden on the state. He told the court that the state had nothing to gain by putting me into prison and that I was remorseful, I had voluntarily sought counseling to try to establish why I made so many mistakes, I regretted my actions and was ashamed of what had happened. My barrister pointed to the gallery and told the judge that I came from a well-loved family and had friends who had supported me every day in court. The judge was then reminded that I was not healthy enough to go to prison; my size would cause me a lot of suffering.

The prosecution, however, wanted a custodial sentence. They felt that I deserved a long sentence, for me abusing the immigration service and wanted to remind the judge that my actions had allowed many people who were illegally in Great Britain now to roam the country. When the judge decided it was his turn to speak the court turned into a morgue. I was prompted to stand up, by my favorite bailiff. I was then given the nod to sit back down. The judge thanked the defense and the prosecuting team. He started to acknowledge my crime and reminded me of the consequences of my actions. He told me that he accepted my previous impeccable record, that I had committed no offense since being arrested. He understood that my size and weight would be a hindrance. I, at that time, thought to myself that my weight may help me out here. Then whilst looking at me he said that big word, that I think everyone was waiting for; but! a crime had been committed and that someone needed to be punished. He continued to say that the court should remember two people had committed these crimes and that only one person was here, to be punished; he told everyone that the other person may never be penalized for what he had done. He, therefore, felt that I should go to prison for two years.

All I heard at that time was my sister and H scream, the rest of the group looked shocked. I just looked over to them. The judge then said, however, because of what he had heard from the defense team, he was happy to suspend any sentence for two years. In a matter of seconds, the sorrow had become cheers. I was free, to go. I thanked the judge, I tried to say more but my barrister prompted me to leave and to be quiet. My family became louder and happier as we started leaving the court building. My barrister questioned the group's behavior and asked "how happy would they have been if I was not given a prison sentence?" I wanted to hug H but could not. H was obviously the happiest. I still wonder now, what H's brother thought of when he heard in court what was being said, about me and his sister. I'm sure he must have thought that this was all for the purpose of the trial.

Because of the uncertainty of any court proceedings, life could not move on financially. It was definably the beginning of the end, of me earning substantial amounts of money. I had now lost the immigration business and could not carry on doing the beer run. My days as a landlord were limited because of the divorce settlement and the so-called splitting of my assets.

Signing on with the police every six weeks, court proceedings concerning money, even custody of the children was all taking its toll. H, through this period was great, she was understanding and patient. She often asked if we were going to get married, or when we were going to get married. At the time I did not think about, it or consider it. There was no reason, why, I just never did. There was no question on custody of the children. Well, from my side there wasn't - however cold she was, I thought U would not give up her children. Although there was no contest on the issue, the barristers had their day, charging me a fortune to tell me that the children were to live with their mother and I had visiting rights, with access to them. Once the court cases concerning the children were resolved, I could put some plans in place.

The trial was finished despite the fact that my barrister was going to appeal. This was irrelevant at the time for me - the only advantage was that if my appeal was successful, I would not have a criminal record. At the time, having a criminal record was the least concern on my mind. The celebrations were over, Plan B concerning the café was not needed but my parents were adamant that they had done enough for me. They had helped me as much as they could. I was now dependent on the cafe as my only income and then another situation that I had not foreseen came about.

Whilst I was in the cafe one afternoon, Gemma rang me through the operator services who asked if I would accept a reverse charge call. My daughter was in a telephone box crying loudly, asking, me if she could come and live with me. She was only twelve years old. I asked her where she was. I told her to go home, she refused. She told me her mother had thrown her out, with her things. I told her to think about what she was saying. She was adamant and hysterical. At the time, my focus was her safety and I wanted her to calm down. I asked where she was then drove like a looney to find her. When I did, she was not wearing a coat and standing by her side was a filled black bin bag. She told me that U had given her the ultimate choice of not seeing her father again, or living with her father. The child chose the latter.   Apparently, whenever I saw Gemma on Sundays, I would take her to church with me and as 'we were supposed to be Muslims' her mother was not willing to allow Gemma to visit a Christian establishment. Without any notice or planning, I was now a single parent. Living at my parent's house was not ideal, but it had to do for the moment. There was not enough room for all of us living in my parents' house, but we made use of what we had. My parents were too tired to be working. I knew if I carried on with the business, they would never retire so as a mark of respect, I put the cafe business up for sale and it was not long before I sold it.

During this period I also was informed by the Court of Appeal that my barrister had convinced the judges that my conviction of corrupting a government official was illegal and that the case had to be canceled and my sentence should be quashed. I was aware that the case was in line to be heard and knew that I did not have to attend. At that time I was slightly relieved, as I no longer had a suspended jail sentence hovering over me. In truth, I felt quite arrogant and chuffed that once again, 'I had got away with it', I had pushed the boundaries, in this case with the system and beat them. It was a case of knowingly being guilty and being allowed to walk free on a technicality. Reflecting on it, did I?

Regina v Naci V Natji Times, 12 March 2002; [2002] EWCA Crim 271
14 Feb 2002
CACD
Lord Justice Mantell, Mr. Justice Bennett, And, His Honour Judge Stephens QC
Crime
The defendant was charged with an offense under the 1889 Act. He had been alleged to have paid an immigration officer for the handing over of certain files which were then destroyed. At trial, the defendant argued that since the officer was an employee of the crown, and the Crown was not a public body within the definition in that Act, the acts did not fall within the 1889 Act, and that he should rather have been charged under the 1906 Act. The 1916 Act extended the definition. Held: The 1916 definition included 'public authorities of all descriptions'

The wording must be checked against the meaning intended at the time, and not by reference to later uses of similar phrases in other Acts. The same 1916 Act, in section 2, drew a clear distinction between the Crown and other public bodies. The Crown was not included in the definition even as amended. The conviction was in error.

Public Bodies Corrupt Practices Act 1889 1(2) - Prevention of Corruption Act 1906 - Prevention of Corruption Act 1916

I now had very little money left. The immigration case and my divorce destroyed me financially. I was now unemployed. I decided I needed a rest and consciously decided to take a break and think about the future. My priority was finding stability for Gemma. I had been given a chance to rent a three-bedroom flat above a shop in Barnet which was clean, cheap but unfurnished. I liked this as now we could decorate and furnish it and make it our new home.

Usain

During this period, my mother had told me that a nephew of hers, Usain, who as far as I knew was living in the northern part of Cyprus, had come to the UK. I always knew this cousin as a young entrepreneur, a risk taker, who could spin anything. I always believed he was doing well in Cyprus but apparently he was not and he had fallen on bad times. After a few inquiries I found out that he was, in fact, working as a kitchen assistant in a very busy cafe in Central London, living with friends and sleeping on their settee. This was a perfect example of "how the mighty had fallen". Usain was cleverer than he thought and if channeled in the right direction, would have been very successful. Usually he was very squeamish and fussy, which is why I was very surprised at hearing that he was doing the washing up in a cafe. He was a very generous person, who had a clean conscience and a good heart. My mother asked me if I could help my cousin to get back on his feet and find him a place to live. I phoned him out of respect to my aunt and offered him the spare room we had in the flat. Usain did not have time to think about it as he was in a desperate state. Before any time had passed he had moved in with me and Gemma.

The shop below our flat was an off license. Usain went downstairs to buy a packet of cigarettes, returned and told me that he had got both of us a job. I looked amazed. He told me that he met a salesman who was selling cash machines or ATMs to stores. This salesman had liked him, thought that Usain could "talk the talk, walk the walk". All Usain wanted from me was for me to drive him around the streets of London, where we would look for and find suitable sites to place ATM cash machines. Usain's job was to convince the owners to install a cash machine in their shop. I would be paid commission on the daily sales. I was happy with what Usain was offering as he was a very good salesman. I was confident in him and he could surely talk a sale. He could convince Eskimos to buy snow, Arabs to buy sand. What did I have to lose? Before I knew it Usain was selling three or four ATMs daily, the concept was great, the idea was great and Usain was very good at his job. The only problem was that when we were going to get paid, the deals were falling through. I had a lot of time to think about the concept, whilst sitting in the car and waiting for Usain to come out of a shop in which he was trying to install a machine. I realized and found out why the deals were not finalizing - the shopkeepers were not getting the finance to buy the machines as they were not passing stringent credit checks. I came up with the idea to find investors who could buy these ATMs and we would install them in these off licenses, small supermarkets, petrol stations and charge customers for withdrawing money from them. The withdrawal fees would then be split three ways; the shop keeper gets a proportion of the withdrawal fee, the rest shared by the machine maintenance company and the ATM Machine owner. On paper a very good idea.

I suggested to Usain that we should find investors who would buy the machines for the shopkeeper and get a proportion of commission. Usain said it was a great idea.

Usain and I decided to set up a company. He did not have any money but I still had some money left over from my divorce. We put in place a business plan and idea. We were now partners. We only needed to install one machine weekly to pay our overheads and get a weekly wage. Instead of spending energy and resources on sites we felt were ideal for a machine, we drove further out of the area, became selective and more thorough. We even recruited other salesmen. I later discovered that Usain was selling more machines than I knew about and had set up another company behind my back with associates of the Turkish mafia who were more financially capable to expand my idea. I was devastated by his betrayal, and very angry. When confronted, Usain denied his deceit saying he did it for me and wanted to surprise me. I told him to vacate my flat and to get out of my life. The partnership was soon dissolved.

A Secret Marriage

In the meantime, my relationship with H was strong but I felt we needed to move up a level. I was struggling with being a lone parent. Gemma was quickly becoming a woman and I did not know how to cope with her periods, her moods and her attitude. She needed a female role model. I thought H would be the one. H always wanted us to get married and at the time I wanted to as well but felt she was not as committed as I was. Whilst waiting for Usain to finish selling a machine in a shop I was sitting in the car listening to the radio, thinking about events, when a song came on playing, "What would you do, if you lose somebody?" I listened to the lyrics and the romantic side of me thought that this was a sign. I immediately rang H and proposed. I did sense some hesitancy but she did say YES.

"Maybe the difference between first marriage and second marriage is that the second time at least you know you are gambling." Elizabeth Gilbert, (I thought this was so true?)

Our wedding day with H quickly came. The wedding was a secret from her parents and H chose not to even tell her oldest daughter Sandra that she was getting married. Sandra was going on holiday at the time and we planned to have the wedding that week. Whilst waiting for H to arrive at the registrar's office I did have it in my mind that she would change her mind and not turn up. She did and we got married.

Gemma and I moved into H's house, which she shared with her three children. Sandra was the other half of H's eldest twins, Eren was the son and Sevinch was the youngest. From day one, I knew I had made another error in my judgment. I sensed that H's children were not happy that someone else had moved into their house, taking over their territory. Sandra definitely was against our marriage.

I now needed to find work. I also needed to get out of the house as it was not healthy staying in the house twenty-four hours a day. H and I would get in each other's way and quarrel over the littlest things. Although at the time the atmosphere in the house was tense, everyone seemed to have accepted the situation. H's children had accepted Gemma as a step sister and the four children seemed to have got on well with each other. I was not seen as a stepfather, but H's husband but felt that Sandra and I were getting on better. It seemed to me she was accepting that I was there and it was nice that she chose to include me in parts of her life. We often spoke about life together, although I was uncomfortable speaking to her, as I did not want to upset her, or say the wrong things. With Eren it was different, he was the son I never had and I tried as much as I could to involve him in my daily activities. With H's youngest child the dynamics were different, as she was a lot younger and attached and closer to her mother. Sevinch, seemed to have not taken too well to the situation and never got used to it.

H seemed happy at the beginning and was very loving towards me. I remember going to the local shops and before I returned the clouds in the sky decided to let go, it was pouring down in rain. Before I had the courage to try and walk home from the shops, H was there outside, with an umbrella. However, the longer Gemma and I lived in H's home, I realized this house was never going to be *our* home. Things had changed, it was now them and us, not me against the world, I had a daughter to think about. It was not a happy home. After about a year, the arguments became louder, more frequent and more aggressive. All the children in the house seemed unhappy and were getting affected. I noticed that Gemma was becoming withdrawn and more alienated. I knew that this new life was not going to last a lot longer, even though I really wanted it to. Gemma was now settled in her new school, I was married for a second time and my ego could not allow me to fail again. I loved H, but I was not happy.

I started at looking into improving my qualifications and felt after what Usain had done to me, I did not want to be self-employed at that present moment. I needed some form of distraction and a way to pass time. Whilst looking at local jobs, I noticed a job vacancy looking for volunteers working and helping people with mental health issues entering employment. As mental health problems were close to my heart, I thought that I would like to do this. I applied and got the position. It was not long that I built up a quick working relationship with the director of the organization, Ms. Claire Downing. In one of our many conversations about self-improving oneself, I think I mentioned that if I had the chance I would like to have gone to university. I told her that I had read a report on how many black and minority ethnic people from the UK went onto University and that I was surprised how low university entrance numbers were for Turkish Cypriots compared with other BME entrants. I also mentioned that if I had gone to university, I would have been a good example to my kids. "If I went to university and got a degree, they would have no excuse, not to follow". Claire's remark was that there was no such thing as "If" and before I knew it I was invited to attend an interview at Goldsmiths University to start a degree in Youth and Community work. H loved this idea, giving me the impression that she was proud of me. She even showed off to others that I was going on to university.

I could not believe it how, within a year, my life had changed. From being a self-employed business man I was going on to university, at the age of forty. Since the age of twenty, I wanted to go to university and now, when I never, ever thought I would ever get the chance, I was actually going to go. I remember going to the interview with my little sister, who was familiar with the university. The chat with the university course leader, Jean Alexandria, went well and she said she believed in me and was willing to take a chance on me. That was a first! Someone was going to give me something that I wanted and it would not cost me anything. I was overjoyed. My sister was waiting outside in the university gardens, sitting on the grass, anxiously waiting for the news of how my interview went. I did not need to tell her how it went - she could see the joy in my body language before I could say anything.

My first day at university was unbelievably one of the better days in my life. I immediately felt that I was, being noticed, I was being listened to, acknowledged. I felt accepted by my peers, and the lecturers who listened to whatever I was saying. My questions were being answered and not being ignored, I was being heard and respected. I quickly became friends with Della, a fellow mature student. Della was a lone parent too, who had an amazing testimony. She spoke about her past and when I heard how she had beaten the odds, and now was in university studying for a degree, it inspired and motivated me even more. She was my backbone for the three years whilst in university. We had a little thing, together, that if one of us was down and ready to give up, the other would step in and remind them why we were there, what had passed, and more importantly, that we were going to wear 'that gown' on graduation day. She was my soul mate.

Della was a great role model. She did not know at the time, how good and how helpful she was to me. My most dramatic and memorable experience whilst in university was during a session of 'group work'. This session was when the whole class would sit around in a circle and discuss an issue, which could be on any subject. I felt that I kept on clashing with a fellow, a peer who was a younger female who, it seemed to me, she disagreed with my opinion just for the sake of it. This happened for the fourth time and I felt that she was undermining me. We were encouraged to learn about challenging situations and I thought this was the moment that I would tell her my thoughts. The girl was shocked and told me that I now had taken away her voice and asked me about the other times I had felt she had undermined me. I looked at her and just waved my hand at her, telling her with my hand gesture, that I was not willing to talk to her anymore. Then Jean, who was facilitating that day, told me she thought I was the most spoilt man that she had ever met. I was shocked and ashamed at the same time, I wanted the ground to open up and swallow me and I felt I had let Jean down. She had given me a chance and I had let myself down on so early into the course. As usual, I felt I was alone again. Me against the rest. I tried to be part of the group but felt that I messed up again. That day and what had happened played a significant role for me, in that I started asking myself, was I that spoilt?

University for me was, from that moment on, becoming the start of my growth, the beginning of my self-development. At the age of forty, life was really starting for me. I started loving this change in me. H never knew ever knew about Della, but she did sense that I was enjoying university too much and I was happy there. I was now interacting with other people, pushing myself, my body to heights I never thought possible. I was walking, talking, taking public transport. I was working towards something on my own. I became prouder of myself daily that I was now not stealing or conning my way for what I wanted. It was not an inheritance. No one was giving it to me. I was working hard for it.

When I came home in the evenings, it was always into an apprehensive environment. H sensed that I was happier when I was at university and she started telling me that I should leave university. It was university or her. I just ignored her at first. H had changed her mind and attitude about the university and we seemed to argue every day. These arguments were turning into fighting. The more I got into my course, the more H wanted me to leave. Then the final day came, the day that would become my last day in the matrimonial home.

Travelling such a long distance from home to university on public transport gave me a lot of time to think about the dynamics of the family home. I came home from university that day and we had a disagreement which escalated into a verbal slanging match. I was getting mentally very tired and arguments were now happening every day. I could see all the children were getting very upset and uncomfortable. I knew it was time to go. One could not avoid the inevitable. I told Gemma to take what possessions she could gather up in a matter of minutes.   We left the home for the last time. I sat in the car, waiting for Gemma to gather her last things and I remember H coming outside and asking me to come back in and talk about it. I did not listen to H as my mind was made up. I now wish that I had listened. I must admit I got it wrong that day and now often wonder, what may have happened if I did not leave that day.

Not even a week had passed and my closest relatives were sending me their condolences for my second marriage ending. I am sure they were all sincere, but many were not surprised. What happened next even stunned me. It was one of those moments that you remember the day, and where you were when something happens. I was in a supermarket car park, walking towards the store and my mobile phone rang. I did not recognize the number. "Hallo, is that Naci?" I said yes. "It's M." came back the reply. "M who? Emine! Wow!" She then apologized for phoning me and explained that she had got my number from my mother and hoped I did not mind. She told me that she would like us to meet and catch up. I remember the conversation word for word. I just listened, because I could not find any words. I could not find anything to say and my mouth and brain just dried up. She told me that she was sorry but she had heard from a cousin of mine that I had recently split from my wife. She wanted to see me. It did not take much thought. I said I would. As usual, I was again wanting, clinging on some sort of hope. H was no longer in my life, I asked myself was this my fate? I still felt that I loved her after two decades and everything was quickly coming back as if it was yesterday. Obviously I never let go fully. I was so weak, and craving for that love. Twenty years had passed but I never really stopped thinking about M although I was getting on with my own life without M knowing it. I went out of my way to find out how M's life was and what was happening. Most of the information learned about M's life was second hand and half accurate, most of it was bad news and about the tragedies in her life. I did not know how to feel when I heard the gossip. Should I still resent her for rejecting me and leaving me in pain for so long? Should I feel bitter maybe, or plan revenge? I do not really know how I felt, only that I was glad to have some sort of connection with her. Now she had phoned me, M asked when we could meet up. I told her I was a free agent. I really did not anticipate why she rang me, all sorts of ideas and thoughts were lingering in my head. She said that she had a flat not far away from my mother's house and I could come round for a coffee. She told me that she had two children and was single, so I could come round to her home that evening. She said that her children go to bed early and we agreed to meet that evening and I went to see her after all those years.

For me, it was as if I was going on a date. I made an effort. When I arrived, I know I was more panicky and anxious than she was. I had feelings and emotions for her but mostly I was nervous about my weight. When she opened the door of her flat, it was as if no time had passed, she was the same small petite little girl I had left two decades ago. We smiled at each other, shared a greeting kiss and I went upstairs. She offered me a drink but I refused. As usual, she commented, whilst laughing that things had not changed. She always had the power over me, I was always too nervous to eat or drink anything in front of her. We spoke about our parents and family and briefly spoke about our children. She spoke about her divorce and I discussed my failed relationships in more detail. She looked very sad and had lost the radiant glow she always had. The last twenty or so years had been hard and it showed. Whilst chatting, the evening's events were broken when a small boy appeared at the doorway of the living room we were sitting in and a little voice just asked "Mummy can I have a cuddle?" "Of course! You can say hello to Uncle Naci, Az," replied M. I looked at Az, and instantly thought to myself, this could have been my son. It was that precise moment that I decided in my head that I needed to write a book. My first thought was the title of the book could be "Mummy can I have a cuddle?"

We talked more about the children, and then innocently - what did M know? - She quickly brought me down to earth and broke my heart once again. Once again, I was still living in a delusion, still dreaming that I would find love on my terms. She told me that she had met someone in Turkey and wanted to bring him to this country and she wanted to talk to me about how he could get a visa. I was instantly broken, I could not believe how insensitive M could be, or that she was that naive. She really did not know. I told her what I knew of the law and what she needed to do before making any applications to the right authorities. She was obviously disappointed with what I told her but she was not aware of how disillusioned I was. I left her home feeling so used. Whilst driving away from M's house, I realized for the first time that I really was in love with H more than any other women. Was it because, at last, I had now found closure after so many years? At that moment in time, I no longer felt anything for M. I asked myself what was this attachment or connection I had with M? Was this the reason I could not really love? I knew there and then I wanted H back so I started thinking, reflecting and blaming myself. I had taken the easy way out, I did not take my marriage seriously or the responsibilities of being married. I had failed as a husband, as a provider and now felt that I had humiliated H by leaving her. I blamed my parents for making it too easy for me to return home. I once again was reminded of how much I hated myself. I hated this body. Would things have been dissimilar if I was different? The pain of not being with H now was starting to hurt badly and I felt guilty for letting H down. This guilt was telling me I needed to do something different in order to repair my relationship with H. It was important for my own self-esteem. Once again I questioned, was this all my fault?

I phoned H and asked her if we could find a way of being together, however little. I was willing to compromise. I had this idea that any little amount of H was better than none of her at all. I convinced her that our relationship could be saved and would remain a secret and I was willing to accept all her terms of a secret romance. I would have accepted anything. The marriage was over but I started to live on that hope and I thrived on believing that one day we would be together. H told me she had too much on her mind at that moment and I had utterly humiliated her. Her relatives had heard that I had left her and said her father was not very well and she needed time with her family. I asked H if it was over between us. She said she did not know and her not knowing always gave me hope. I lived on that hope. We were apart for about three months but spoke on the phone. Again I felt there was still something between us. H's father soon got worse and passed away. I knew the last thing that H needed was me and the problems that came with our relationship. I did not go to H's father's funeral, as H had requested I stayed away. I never questioned why, I just respected her wishes. I was always scared of cemeteries and death, so it was not a bad thing. We spoke on the phone during this time a lot and eventually H allowed me back into her life. I did sense that H had lost herself and in that few months we were apart she had deteriorated. She was a broken person. She had lost her beloved father. She was still grieving and I found it hard to talk to her. I just listened more, became very passive and most of the time became the weaker one of the couple.

When I was with H we often spoke about her father and how much she missed him. I understood her, as I knew what a good man he was, what a great father he was and how much H loved her father. One day, out of the blue, whilst driving past the cemetery where he lay, I decided to combat my fears and go and pay my respects to him. After the first time other visits became easier and I often bought flowers to put on his grave. I used to sit and talk to him for hours sometimes, telling him what I was up to, asking him to forgive me for loving his daughter and causing him shame and embarrassing him. I kept on telling him how much I loved H. H would often laugh, when her mother queried, who the stranger was putting flowers on her husband's grave. Although H never got over her father's passing, she knew things were never going to be the same from then on. I accepted that when H's father died, a big part of her died also.

I was now entering the last year of my university degree. I also needed to find somewhere for me to live, as living with my parents again could not be permanent. H and I always discussed buying a holiday home and I always wanted to live in front of the sea, so I made my mind up and started house hunting, I kept it a secret from everyone, especially H. I was still entitled to the student loan, which would help with the mortgage payments until I found work, I had the deposit, so why not. I saw a nice flat in East Sussex on the sea front. When the estate agent was showing me the flat, I fell in love with the view in front of the building. I did not bother, or want to see the other rooms. The estate agent laughed at my enthusiasm and of course I bought it. H was constantly nagging, and telling me that I was wasted and that I should improve myself and not waste my university degree. I now needed to look into finding a job.

I had already completed the required dissertation for that final year and knew that I would have plenty of time in the forthcoming year, so I applied for a job in the local council as a support worker. Firstly I did not know what a support worker was and what the job entailed, I just felt it was a start. I had planned to work at this post for a year and when I graduated, I could find the appropriate job that I was trained for. I got the job and when I joined New Opportunities I really, truly did not know what I was really going to do. I never understood the true meaning of what was required of a support worker. If you asked some of my work colleagues, they would still say that I do not know what a support worker's role is. Well, that is just their opinion. I was thrown into the deep end straight away. I had never heard of personal care, not about carrying it out on another person. I was not squeamish, but queasy enough to be repulsed by it. The job meant that I was now earning a regular income. In the first year at New Opportunities it was no surprise that I did not take the job seriously and my 'laid back' attitude was quickly clocked. I instantly became friends with Tom Ford, who was a long time employer of the organization.

Tom Ford would often remind me of my inappropriate behavior at work and that I was pushing boundaries far too quickly and too often. At the time, I did not really care and told Tom Ford how I felt within myself, that I was untouchable because I was dead. Tom Ford never gave much away so I never knew how he felt about that. Anyway, it did not sound good but I knew I was paid to be a carer, but I did not care. I did the job solely for the money and no other reason. I had no reason to care, I had flaunted a fortune, I was losing the one I loved, I had no respect for myself and loathed myself. I was a dead man walking!

Divorcing for Christmas

When I took H to see the flat for the first time she loved it. The flat would now be our holiday home and every four or six weeks, we would drive down to East Sussex to the flat. Life was ideal, the arrangement suited H and I could still see H. I successfully completed my degree and graduated and I was content with this situation. However H soon started talking about divorcing me more and more, although she assured me that nothing would have changed between us, and that we loved each other; our marriage was only on paper and meant nothing, She never admitted why she wanted the divorce, but I had my suspicions. She told me that we could never ever be together as man and wife, she was not willing to lose another parent over me and that I would never understand because both my parents were still alive. It was then I knew and accepted that the pendulum had swung. I was now becoming the obsessive one in this relationship and being in this marriage meant something to me. I belonged to someone, I was a husband to somebody, she was carrying my name and someone loved me. One by one H was removing these labels that I had held onto and it started to hurt more and more. I could not get my head around it. Was this H's way of letting me down gently and was it, really over?

H had her reasons that were her own and I was in a predicament. I had no choice but to agree. I knew that H had the legal system on her side as I had left the matrimonial home for over five years. I knew she would divorce me, one way or the other and I suspected that her mother paid the legal fees to divorce me. Once again I felt rejected. I had lost the battle and the war and could only hang onto the little I had left with her. I could not stop her or change her mind. It was not long, the legal paperwork from the courts had come through for me to sign and to accept that my second marriage was over. I avoided signing the forms as long as I could but decided to sign and post them on Christmas day 2007 for two reasons, one was to hurt myself, or 'self -harm' as a professional psychologist would say. Secondly, I phoned H, who I knew was working on that day, to tell her that I had given her the divorce she wanted, without any resistance. I told her that I had signed the papers and put them in a post box. I wanted her to feel some grief, just a little, if any. Things are still vague and blank. I still cannot memorize what she had said but I do remember tears running down my face. I was feeling tired of trying, sick of crying, but I knew inside I was dying.

That Christmas day I was expected to drive to Kent to spend the day with the extended family. Driving to Kent, although in a full car with my parents and daughters, was the loneliest sixty miles I had ever driven in my life. My cousin had invited over thirty guests that day to celebrate this festive day but I was there physically. Mentally and spiritually I was somewhere else. People spoke to me but I looked at them through tear-filled shiny eyes but nobody knew the pain I was in. To add to my pain, Usain was invited to the Christmas festivities. When I saw him, it was hard to ignore him. As much as I tried, Usain was not going to allow it. He reminded me that it was Christmas, and a time of forgiveness. I was weak and vulnerable and very low, so whatever Usain said to me was not going to register. I just nodded, shook hands, and that was the end of that. He told me how he was now a CEO in an ATM distribution company and he was going to take the idea to Turkey. He had involved himself with a Turkish business man and they were willing to invest in his ideas. I just thought, things have not changed. You still are a fraud. Those ideas were my ideas. Usain may have forgotten that I knew that he had been associating and working with the Turkish Mafia, so when I heard from him about his partners, I did get scared for him.

Memories of my court case flowed back. I was still sleeping with my bedroom door open, with the lights left on. So this was one time I was not envious. My attitude was that of good luck. It was not long that stories and gossip on the Turkish grapevine were growing, that Usain had set up a business in Turkey and had become very rich, extremely quickly and he was in partnership with a very influential financier in the banking world who was very well respected. He had managed to sell my 'idea' to other Turkish businessmen who were willing to invest in it. At the time, I thought to myself that this was typical Usain, he would take someone else's ideas and manage to convince investors. In all his past business ventures Usain was not too successful. Was this the one that Usain would make good? Usain was coming to the UK on a business trip and he planned to visit my mother's house for a visit, so of course, he would be showing off. This was his style. My mother asked me to be there and that I should not show any animosity. She told me not to hold any grudges and not show him that I was still upset. My mum thought that Usain would see this as me being envious of his success.

Usain came to us, arms full of gifts, all for my mother. We sat to eat and he started telling us how he had helped an old friend that we both knew. He explained that this friend of ours phoned him, told him that his girlfriend had thrown him out and he was homeless and penniless. Usain paid for him to fly to Turkey. On his arrival to Istanbul, our friend had become very underweight and looked unwell. After a few weeks, Usain ordered tailors to make him three sets of suits and shirts. They trained him, gave him free accommodation, and now this friend was one of the company's best salesmen. I listened and then picked up my ears; desperation and weakness was taking over. Was this a way out of being a support worker, a new career? If I was successful, H would have been happy. I could feel my vulnerability and desperation. The next day Usain planned that he and his partner were going to the sales at the local shopping center. Usain asked me if I wanted to go with them.

I took this opportunity to ask Usain if there was any chance that he could do what he did for our friend, for me. I told him how unhappy I was at that moment. The first thing he said to me was that a man of my size would have no chance of surviving in Turkey. If I felt victimized in the UK for being overweight, it would be ten times worse in Turkey. Usain continued to tell me that he felt he owed me and wanted to repay me. He told me he had made contacts in Turkey, he knew of doctors who specialized in Bariatrics and that he would pay for me have a gastric bypass. His girlfriend even commented that she would nurse and support me with my recovery. I hung on to what they both said and immediately started my plan to go to Turkey to see what it would be like and if it was feasible. This could be the answer to my dreams - a new career and a new life.

ISTANBUL

I took annual leave from work and went to Turkey with H's blessing. This was my first time in Istanbul. Usain came with his chauffeur to the airport to greet me. He introduced me to his chauffeur and instructed him immediately to help me and look after me. I was called Sir. Usain also gave me keys to an apartment and I was taken there. First impressions looked very impressive. Usain was clearly in charge, he could not have welcomed me more generously. There was a swimming pool, gym and sauna, in the compound where my apartment was and it was only a walk away from the office where Usain was operating his businesses. That was one of the few times I was going to see Usain. When we arrived in Sisli, which at the time I did not know would be my home for almost six months, Usain left me with the chauffeur, who introduced himself to me as Ugur and he asked me what my relationship with Mr. Usain was. I told him and Ugur told me that Mr. Usain must either loved me a lot or really had a lot of respect for me as he never left his office for anyone. For him to come and greet me at the airport, I must have been special. I just nodded and listened. The longer I was there Ugur gave me information about Usain's business. I found out that Usain was working on a number of projects. He was working on a gambling idea, which he thought of. He was also very close to bringing to Turkey a fast food franchise of a famous spiced chicken restaurant. I liked what I saw and felt happy and started to believe that this could work. I began a diet regime, started to use the gym and the swimming pool.

Usain ordered in his tailors and paid for me to have made to measure clothes. He instructed his chauffeur to take me shopping to buy suitable footwear. Early every morning, I would avoid any onlookers and use the swimming pool. It was a refreshing start to the day. Then I'd dress in my professional outfit and show my presence in the office. About two weeks after arriving in Turkey I heard again from Ugur that Usain had flown to South Africa to talk about the chicken business. When Usain returned back from South Africa, he sent me a message via Ugur, that he was inviting me for dinner that evening, with his girlfriend. This was the first time in two weeks that I had a chance to catch up with him apart from when we met up at the airport. I started to doubt my future, so having dinner with him was not only 'catch up' but also to discuss my future. Once again I started feeling weak, wanting and vulnerable. That evening Usain apologized for his scarce appearances and told me this was the way it was.

His girlfriend had ordered a Chinese takeaway that night, but she made soup herself. Usain had brought back from South Africa examples of the products he was going to promote with the chicken restaurant. He brought with him a triple xxx chili sauce which was not available yet elsewhere in the world. I was a lover of hot sauce and put some in my soup. The sauce was very hot but nice. That evening went well and I understood Usain's role, accepted his position and got the impression that Usain was not as powerful or influential as we all thought. It was disappointing, but I got the feeling that Usain was more of a puppet and that someone else was in control. I left Usain's apartment that night more confused than when I went in.

I thought to myself, that I could not give up my job in London. Usain had not given me the confidence to make my life in Istanbul. I went back to my apartment and sat down to think of my options. I thought about H and her shattered illusion, of me becoming a successful businessman, about returning back to the role of a support worker. I fell asleep in the armchair that I was sitting in. I found myself waking, in the middle of the night, very thirsty. I thought that the chili sauce that I tried the evening before had made me very dry. I tried to drink some bottled water but found as I was drinking from the bottle, I could not hold the water in my mouth and the water was gushing back out, I could not close my lips. At the time I thought it was just a reaction from the spicy sauce. I then went to bed. When I woke in the morning, the right side of my face felt numb and I noticed when I looked at myself in the bathroom mirror that my face had collapsed on the right side. I got the shock of my life, I thought I was having a stroke. I phoned the office looking for Usain but he was not available. I told the receptionist my situation and she told me she would contact Ugur, who would help me. Ugur came as quickly as he could and took me onto the local hospital. When I arrived at the hospital, the emergency department rushed me through the corridors to an examination room. The medication staff did not want to waste any time. They did not even bother to ask my name. I heard them say to Ugur that I had had a facial stroke and it was good that I got to the hospital as quick as I did. I had, in fact, had Bell's palsy.

I was prescribed steroid treatment and told to rest and not fly for at least eight weeks. I started getting scared, not only for my health, but also worried about work in London, not to mention my future plans which had been destroyed. I was fortunate that I had taken out medical insurance and I felt secure and safe, knowing the doctors were competent. A week after I got unwell, I visited a consultant who told me the Bell's Palsy had been brought on by a very bad ear infection that I had most probably picked up from the local swimming pool. He looked at my ear and told me I needed a minor operation to clear the infection. This was done immediately and I was told that I should not take a chance and fly for at least four months.

I had not seen Usain since the first day when I got ill. He came and visited me in my apartment that day but he did not look happy himself. He looked worried, he was not himself. I remember him commenting to me, saying "there were more important things in life than being ill." I thought that was rather insensitive but was too weak to ask him what he meant. The next three months were very lonely for me. I spent most of the time in the apartment on my own, on social networks. I made a lot of new friends, but one I especially became friends with was Lynda who is still my friend now. Lynda and I spoke for hours. We even swapped telephone numbers and texted each other daily. Lynda and I have a special friendship, in that we have never ever spoken to each other verbally. She is a great mentor and a listener. And yes, she is a blonde. Lynda helped me through that period, and I could say, she kept me sane through this stage. I did not ever mention to her that I was recovering from an illness. The terms of our friendship have not changed so many years down the line.

Fortunately, I was still being paid my full salary at work in London, so my extended holiday allowed me to get to know the surrounding areas well. I went out for long walks but these trips out were always spoilt by me being very conscious about my facial deformity. My disfigured face also was another reason for not wanting to return back to England. I did not want H to see me this way.

It was obvious that I was not going to be staying on in Turkey, however much I grew to love the country. I felt like I had found my identity in Istanbul. I did not feel alienated from its people, I felt I was one of them. They did not care if you were fat, or disfigured, contrary to what Usain had once told me. Once I felt I was getting better, I found the courage to go and visit people I had made friends with in the offices. I knew my days were numbered and it was a way of letting people know that I was soon leaving and how I would miss them. I was fortunate to see Usain's office door opened so I took this opportunity to say hello. He did not look happy. I thanked him for everything he had done for me and said I was disappointed we couldn't have spent more time together. I told him I needed to go back to London and that I was sad that things did not work out but did not have any regrets. Usain then once again said something that I felt was odd and did not understand. He told me "that everyone gets what they deserve". I was puzzled and when I left his office tried to understand what he meant. Was he pointing out that I deserved my illness? Did I not do enough to justify a job in his company?

Paranoia started to play tricks in my mind. I did not feel well enough and was anxious about my return to London but arranged to leave as soon as I could. I now had to tell H and the rest of my family of what had happened to me. My face was still disfigured. I did not know what to expect, how H would react. My mother, how will she be? These are the moments when people say: "Only your mother will cry over you". I did feel disappointed when I boarded the plane to return back to the UK. Another dream was shattered. When I left the UK, I was hoping to be starting a new career, a new life style, even a new me. It was not to be, I should have been grateful that I was alive, was the Bell's palsy a wakeup call?

I had returned back to London and it was as if I had never left. I got on the underground train once outside the airport and was now heading home back, to what I had left behind. I picked up a free newspaper, discarded by another reader from the ground. I boarded the train, sat down to read it, as I had another two hours traveling before I would be home. I could not wait to see H. I felt I had in a way, let her down. She would have wanted me to stay in Istanbul and make a success of it. As expected my mother was quite shocked when she saw my face for the first time. She burst out crying, and as expected, it hit me, more then, than when I was alone in Istanbul. I still spoke with a drunken slur and had to be more careful when I ate. It was more obvious when I tried to laugh as my lips could not function together. I started thinking that the elephant man had returned.

BEGINNING OF THE END

I spoke to H on the phone, and met her that evening. I drove to pick her up from work. Her life had not changed in the last five months. It was as if nothing had happened. Life was now back to reality. About three months after returning to the UK, the honeymoon period was over. I had returned to full time work, life was getting back to its monotonous ways, H and I were still struggling to stay together and I started seeing more cracks and strains in our relationship. I felt that H was losing patience with me, she was not happy and I felt I was struggling to keep hold of her. I knew this relationship boat was still sinking fast and I was the only one rowing.

By this time my little sister had got engaged to a man she had met whilst working in Dubai. She had rung me out of the blue and told me that she and her future husband were in London and would I like to meet her fiancé. I met P in a very posh, luxurious hotel near Marlborough and she introduced me to Yusuf, His Excellency. She smiled proudly at me when she declared those two words; 'His Excellency'. I felt my immature, stupid mode kick in but I tried to suppress it. I looked him up and down in my mind as I asked myself what an elder brother is supposed to do in these situations. First of all, I did not know what 'His Excellency' really meant. I just shook his hand. I really did not know what to expect, or how I was supposed to behave. This was my future brother-in-law! I was now sitting down, drinking a cup of coffee at the Landmark Hotel and we started talking about life in general. I told him I was a lone parent with two daughters. I tried to keep the conversation as brief as I could, looking at my little sister as I spoke, in case I said something out of place. I did not want to embarrass her. Then surprisingly, he suggested finding me a wife from Syria. "She will bathe you, cook for you, and kiss your feet!" I just laughed at the situation, thinking to myself, I'm drinking a £20 cup of coffee in a 5 star hotel and this bloke, who is an 'Excellency' that I have just met, is telling me, that he is going to find me a wife. He obviously did not know who he was talking too, he did not realize how screwed up I was mentally. I nodded for the sake of it. He did not know that I was with H, the love of my life. Of course, he did not, how could he know? I knew at that moment of time no other women would or could give me what H had given me but no one could have understood why I still wanted her, I could not comprehend it myself. Without knowing it, Yusuf planted a seed in my head. The bells started ringing again in my head, could this be it? I was still desperately unhappy and hanging onto the dream of improving my situation, ultimately convincing H that I could give her the life she wanted. I could get a job abroad, I was now becoming more experienced in my field and I knew a lot about autism and learning disabilities. Why not go abroad as a consultant, or even teach? Maybe Yusuf's chat with me was 'hot air' for him but I hung onto what he suggested, asking myself why not?

I rushed into it. I put my research hat on and looked into getting a recognized teaching qualification. I found out that this would only take a year, why not? So that is what I did. I started a course to become a teacher. H thought it was a great idea once again as she was always nagging me to improve myself and not waste my time as a carer.

The following year, was the year that my little sister was to marry her prince. She loved the Landmark hotel and decided that she would have her wedding reception there. It was a great day, as weddings go. It was an alcohol-free wedding as Yusuf was a practicing Muslim and did not want alcohol served at the reception. My little sister expected me to read a speech, on her behalf. Well, I was standing in front of two hundred guests, telling the world how happy I was that my little sis was getting married to this 'Prince' was not going to be easy. However with the aid of a bottle of Louis Roeder Carte hidden in the hotel room that my little sis had earlier reserved for me to get prepared in and to stay that night, reading the speech was easier than I expected. I invited H to come to the wedding and would have loved her to have come but she chose not to, saying it would have been impossible for reasons only she will know. The wedding and its preparations became a temporary distraction to my unhappiness and depression. My insecurities were dampened but being with H was still a burden and a heavy weight on our shoulders, maybe more for her than me, but we still held on.

I passed my exams and became a qualified teacher. I decided to specialize in teaching health and social care with the intention of going to the United Arab Emirates to teach. H and I discussed my plans and I felt it was my plans rather than our plans. I sensed that H was happy for me to move on but had become tired, maybe of me, my fantasies or she had just had given up on us. At the time my gut instinct told me it was over but I did not want to believe it or accept it.

Soon after the wedding, my little sister became a mother. She had a little girl, another female grandchild for my parents. I started liking the fact that eventually I was being recognized and had another label. I was now an uncle. My first niece was a joy in my life and instantly became part of it. I booked a month off to visit the UAE as a holiday to see the baby and to find out if I could get a job and live there.

H and I planned to spend the last weekend together at the flat before I went to the UAE. We arrived at Hastings earlier than usual on that last Saturday as there was not much traffic. Before we went to the flat, we thought we would both have an Italian meal together. It was our first time together in that particular restaurant and it was an unusual experience, for me, anyway. Without any planning, we were very blunt with each other and discussed and agreed that our relationship was not making either of us happy. We both agreed that this could not continue. It was like a business meeting, negotiating our future together. I told her what I thought she wanted to hear. By this time she was quickly getting drunk on a bottle of red wine. I was sober as I still had to drive home. I told her about me living abroad, coming to the UK every two months, and asked if we could see each other. H seemed to love the idea. We even shook hands on it, which was rather formal. At the time it all seemed civil and amicable. I ordered another bottle of wine and H got drunk, so I had to help her walk to the car. She did like a drink, but I had not seen her drink so fast and to get drunk so quickly for a long time. We went back to the flat and as I remember it, had a great loving weekend. I did not recognize anything different on our way back to London. I drove, H slept most of the way, interrupting her sleep to have a cigarette. The closer we got to her house, the more frequently she would light up. We parted as usual and we said our goodbyes. I did not feel that anything was wrong; I said that I would try to telephone her when I got to Abu Dhabi. I was sad that I was leaving, but thought of our future. More desperate measures on my behalf to try and win H's heart back.

Abu Dhabi was as expected. I was treated like royalty for my stay, my little sister and Yusef being very generous with their time and hospitality. My little niece had grown and was the cute baby I was expecting. I felt the country was a bit of a letdown but I felt it had enough potential for me - I could have lived there if I had to. Finding a job was more complicated than I had

121

anticipated. The myth of expats finding work in UAE was not as straight forward as I expected. I phoned H a few times and she did not give me any indication of I would be confronting when I went back to the UK. All the times I spoke to H she never gave any indication of any problems.

When I returned to London, I waited a few days before I phoned H. She did not reply to any of my phone calls. I could not concentrate at work so I would sneak to the staff toilets and telephone her. When she did eventually answer her first words to me, were "Had you not got the message?" I asked her what she meant by that. Before she could answer, I asked her, quietly and submissively, "Are we finished?" She continued to tell me that in the few weeks that I was away she did not miss me and that she had realized she could live without me. She had too much going on in her life to carry on in this complicated relationship, she now felt so free, no longer having to hide, or have this secret in her life. I struggled to take in what she was saying. I tried to be understanding but obviously did not want to finish the relationship this way, but deep down in my sadistic way I felt the same, I did not miss her when I was away, but I was so scared of a life without her I did not want her to end the relationship. I would have preferred to have finished it off, myself, my way.

The next thirty hours were so lonely and I found myself crying all the time and could not sleep. I tried to block out what I knew – it was the end. This was M all over again. Feeling rejected. I remember the next Saturday evening I set the alarm on my phone to go off at 7.30am, not the usual 6.00am, rolled myself into a ball and tried to force myself to sleep. I found myself constantly talking and asking God to take away this pain that I was in. I was not religious but still believed in a God and found myself for the first time in a long time chatting to him. I always had the attitude that it was selfish to ask for things from God in prayers, contradicting what most churches try to teach. Asking God for what you want whilst praying was meant to be normal. I was never comfortable with that thought. I was so lost. I questioned my worthiness for God to be listening to me. I would naturally wake and glance at the clock throughout the night thinking and a part of me was hoping, maybe H would ring me and ask for a lift to work. I felt like a criminal who had just been released out of prison, after completing a lifelong prison sentence. Although I was free, I did not know what to do with myself. I now knew the feeling and the meaning of the word; institutionalization. I was misplaced, what was I going to do now, especially in the mornings? I had lost my job driving H, my best friend, back and forward to work. I felt valueless. I had got used to doing this unconventional life. It was part of me being of use.

My so-called loved ones did not understand. They believed that H was using me; I was wasting my time and money driving back to Romford, then Chigwell and then home every day, 6 o'clock in the morning, snow, rain and shine for over 5 years. I knew what my family was thinking, calling me a 'mug' behind my back. They thought H was exploiting me, taking advantages of my weaknesses and soft heart. Most of the time I felt the same but now saw things their way. How was I going to get through this? In the evenings when I was supposed to do that journey picking H up from work and then going home again, it was easier. I would cover up this void by going to the betting shop more and escaping into the mind of those computerized fruit machines. On Saturdays, if I had any money left, I would go to the casino and engulf my thoughts around a roulette wheel. My soul and spirit would transcend into these gambling mechanisms like they would swallow me up. I felt like I was turning with the silver ball, or that I was part of the virtual screen of the computer gambling terminal. I was wasting all my money and time.

Twenty-one days had passed since leaving Abu Dhabi and I was counting every second. I started to very slowly accept that the relationship between H and I was over. I started to play mind games and reflect. I compared the relationship to that of a couple who were together, but the other one was dying of a terminal illness; we both knew that one day it would have to end but stayed together to that final day, tormented with the knowledge there was no future together and it will come to an end. I felt that H was the one who had died and I was the one left to grieve. I wish that the roles were reversed. It would have been less painful. I now had the rest of my life ahead of me, now without my loved one, my soul mate. She was gone. Maybe this metaphor was something I made up to soften the blow of losing someone once more. Was I in denial?

All I knew was the hurt and great pain I was going through from my loss. On a good day I knew deep down I was now free from any further pain. On a bad day it was bad. Suicidal thoughts and voices started to come into my head. It would only have got worse if I found out that H had given me up for someone else, or if she was with someone else now. I was hurt but now had the freedom of not having to work extra hours, driving up and down the A406, no need to find money to put diesel in the car to take H back and forth to work, or give her money for things she always asked for. I now did not have to get up in the mornings, or break up my day in the evenings. I could now live for myself, not around H and her life. I could now take risks or chances, take up a new career, anywhere in the world. I knew all of this but I was very unhappy. In fact, I felt literally very sick that it was finally over.

Moving on

My mental state and depression started to became more obvious to me. I could now spend more time on myself now that I had now lost my major distraction. It had up to now been personal but my miserable condition now became a family issue and as soon as I went home I argued constantly with my parents. I had not had a good relationship with my mother for years and we had drifted apart over the past fifteen years. She often said that I had no respect for her and she had lost a son when I got married to U. For a joke, I used to call her a Fattest as she was obsessed with me losing weight. I know that I often joked about it but I felt she did not like fat people. Both my parents knew something was wrong and started questioning me on why I was behaving the way I was. My mother questioned me on my health, constantly asking if I was ill. My father was not that concerned, he more or less just assured me that whatever was bothering me, I should not worry, because I had a roof over my head. I eventually told them why I was unhappy and what had happened. Mother was relieved and didn't hide her delight. She did not like H anyway, never forgiving her for the way she had treated me in the past.

Other members of my family and some friends, those who knew about H and what the relationship was about, one by one started to tell me I was now liberated and that H was not good for me. My eldest daughter did not hide her joy. She hated H with a passion and often told me that I was too good for H and that I could easily find someone else. When I told my close friend and mentor, Leslie of what had happened, then commented, that I had now 'lost', he disagreed and quiet poignantly said "No, you have won". This was quite profound as Leslie was not a person to judge, or be unfair. When Leslie said anything to me I respected it. I did not know why this was so, maybe because I appreciated his academic achievements. Whenever Leslie said anything to me, I would always try and analyze and take in whatever he said and in this instance I did so again. My sister also, who was a bit withdrawn on the subject of my relationship with H, told me that I could not have done any more for H. I had done more than I could to remain in the relationship and keep it alive. The first week had passed and I was quite proud of myself for how I was coping.

Xmas 2011 was quickly approaching and I was entering my sixth year at New Opportunities. I was now settled as a public official, working for my local council. The job of Community Support Worker was now my final job title. I could not see myself ever having a career change. I was now in what the pessimist would call a dead end job, no promotional prospects, no chance of any wage increases. The optimist would say I had a secure job, fairly well paid, with many advantages, good sickness benefits and a healthy pension, although the last was irrelevant as it never came into my consideration that I would ever live to reach a pensionable age. I think I would have liked to have agreed with the optimist's view. Work was, at times, one of the happiest periods in the last five or so years but now it was all over for me. I hated Mondays so much, it made me ill. I called it 'Mondayitis'.

Work used to be a place where I could escape and be a valued person and be respected. I started to feel irritable and sensitive. I became invisible again. Parents and other carers or even other professionals who visited the center would 'assume' that I had a learning disability and that I was one of the service users. On more than one occasion when I answered the door of the center, the person would look me up and down, turn on the patronizing voice and ask if there were any members of staff available. Even when I told them I was part of the staff the person smiled at me and again repeated their request for a staff member. On one occasion, I was seeing off a male Occupational Therapist after we had a meeting together with one of my clients. The OT was signing out when the doorbell rang. I answered the door to see a person delivering a large brown envelope and I greeted the man and asked what he wanted. He told me he wanted to deliver the envelope. I offered my hand to take the envelope but the person was reluctant to give it to me. The deliveryman then turned his attention to the OT and started to talk to him about the envelope. The OT told the man that he did not work there. I then told the delivery man that he could leave the envelope with me but this was ignored. I then became assertive and asked the delivery man if I was not big enough and could he not see me? He then gave me the envelope. The OT had realized that I was upset and told me that I should ignore other people's ignorance. I was happy that the OT had witnessed my experience and that being invisible was not all down to my paranoia. The only thing worse than me being hated was being ignored. Rejected. The feeling that I didn't exist was not a feeling I enjoyed.

In an interesting way I was sometimes happy to be associated and be labeled as a service user, because sometimes I would rather have been a part of group in the community who were innocent and knew no evil, than one of these so-called professionals, who were sometimes judgmental and hypocrites, who should have known better. I quickly recognized that I only did this job for its financial gain. I felt guilty within myself, because I felt that the major quality needed for this job was to be to a natural carer, which I felt I was not. I felt that the job grew with me over the years and I just got better at it. Even though working helped in paying the bills, the job often reminded me of my failures to look after all the money that I had earned in the past. I was tormented, mentally when money was running low in my bank account. As each year passed, I was getting poorer quicker into the month, waiting for the next payday. I was constantly reminded of how I had changed from a landlord, running many successful businesses, to working for the council as a glorified babysitter. When I was with H, she often said that she hated the job I was doing and she often queried when I would be using be qualifications to better myself. She often used to ask me why did I go to university and end up a carer like herself. I could not disagree with her opinion, or justify my changes in circumstances.

In my second year as a Support worker, because of my Youth Work qualification, I was asked by my manager if I was interested in being part of the council offering respite to parents on Saturdays and few hours on one or two nights a week. The plan was to create a Youth Club for Autistic Children who were in transition from childhood to becoming an Adult. I quickly, without any thought, accepted the manager's proposition. This was a chance for me to earn more money. H was my main reason and my motivation to earn more money. I did, however, feel privileged and happy with myself that the management offered me the chance to become club coordinator for the council's new project. At last, I could use my university degree to some purpose. It was the first time that my three years at University paid some reward. I remembered at this time what my dad had said to my little sister when they were witnessing me at my Graduation Ceremony that I was now 'Employable'. It was not often my father paid me a compliment.

Now that I did not have H in my life I did not have the motivation to carry on working those extra hours. I was lost and did not know what to do with myself. I had become more became miserable and my depression was getting worse. It was getting harder for me to hide pain. Every person around me had noticed this and was constantly asking me about my health. I soon went into free-fall and blamed H for ending our relationship. I carried on with my excessive eating and gambling and this time I noticed that I was really going through bad cravings, either to eat chocolate or to gamble. I had for a long time been saving to buy H a designer bag and I remember being so angry and frustrated. I wanted revenge and my thought was to use H's bag money to enjoy myself. Well, it was not long before I had lost all the money that I had saved in the H bag fund. Running out of money controlled my gambling disorder, but funny as it may sound I did not care about the money, I had lost. It was my eating problem.

I was eating to oblivion, eating so much until I could not physically walk. Being bloated was an everyday thing. I was back to my old ways, I could not cope. I now knew it was time to stop everything. Once and for all. I was now eating foods that I knew were high in fat, such as chips and Doner kebabs. I then would take medication that separated the consumed fats in my body then discharged it. I had become a human oil refinery. Every time I had a bowel movement I was excreting so much oil, I could have powered a diesel engine. My downward plummet was in avalanche mode, I was sinking. I was now on an unconscious suicide mission, killing myself slowly but surely. I kept on trying to convince myself by saying to myself that H was not a bad person, she was not to blame for my state. The question in my head and that started to hurt the most was the thought that I meant nothing to her. The last few years were made up of me giving her everything. Her taking and giving less and less back. I then I started thinking of suicide more and more. Let me get it over and done with! I want to die! How I was going to do it? I renamed Mondayitis and it became Suicide Monday. I was finding myself staring out of the window in work in a daze, slowly sinking into 'I'm the victim here' thinking. I started calling Mr. Depression to come into me and to take over my body. I am worthless! I want to die!

In the last forty-five years I had never really lost any weight, however much my mother wanted me to or tried to make me. For a couple of months, I might lose a few pounds, but would then put double the weight back on. My mother always said that the problems I had in life were because of my weight. She was not the only one who thought that I think, though her concern was my health as she did not know everything about me. In a way, I had to agree with her but never liked to admit it. I believe most of the disappointments in my life were consequences of my addiction to food. The cost was visible - this obese and colossal body that I had developed and accumulated over half a century. It took me about thirty five years to realize that I was fat, really fat! It may have been denial, or I was just too stupid to see it myself. When I did start to accept that I was a big man, I started to hate my body. Seeing myself in the nude repulsed me. It was soon after that I realized that I was also wounded mentally. I remember watching for the first time a film starring Al Pacino, "Scent of a Woman" in the mid 1990's, where Pacino plays a blind, blunt and ultimately compassionate retired ex-army character called Lieutenant Colonel Frank Slade. In one scene he is about to kill himself and he tries to justify why he wants to die by shouting out the words "I'm in the dark here!" Well, my unhappiness was because I could understand and identify with that emotion. Although I could physically see, I was mentally blinded. My body was holding me back. Most importantly it was draining

130

my confidence and suppressing my ego. It had made me what I was and I could not see any way out. I was constantly making the same mistakes, gambling, eating too much, being irresponsible and I could not find any answers.

To entertain my misery, I started playing games again. At work, a new acting team leader was appointed, because one of the usual ones had taken a career break for a year. I applied for the vacant position but because of the fear of being rejected I withdrew my application for that role. It turned out that Andrew, an external applicant, got the job. I do not know why, as he really was a nice person, but I decided from the first day that I would push boundaries with him from the start. He did not deserve it, and although he seemed to be doing a good job, my challenging behavior, deliberately pushing him, made him make errors, very early on. I do not know if Andrew's work performance was not good enough for the position, but he did not stay in the post as long as needed. I still to this day, ask myself, why I acted the way I did to give him such a bad time. Was my life that boring, was I that unhappy?

I would go home after work, miserable and sad, and pick a fight with my parents, more so with my father. Reminding him of his failures as a father, contradicting myself constantly, one minute I would blame him for being too soft on me and making me rely on him; spoiling me, by always offering me a home to come back to whenever I messed up and felt the pressures of life. He always told me not to worry, if any one upset me, I should tell them where to go. I used this attitude throughout life and it had got me nowhere. I blamed him for introducing me to gambling. We were fighting almost every night, words were exchanged that I never imagined my father and I saying, such hurtful words to each other. The fights became regular and after another bad, vulgar, slanging match, I thought it was time

131

to leave home before more spiteful and hurtful words were said. That day I decided to leave.

I sat in the car because I had nowhere to go. My poor mother became hysterical, she told me to come back into the house but too much had been said, it was time for me to leave. I drove away not knowing where I was going. I drove into a 24-hour supermarket car park, parked up and cried myself to sleep. It was cold that night, very cold. I had an old sleeping bag that I always kept in the boot, in case I ever broke down on the motorway and that night, it came into use. I woke up many times. It was one of the worst nights I could remember. I woke very early, walked into the supermarket and used all the facilities. I bought some toiletries and discreetly freshened up. I waited for the cafe to open and bought myself a pot of tea and drunk it in a few gulps. I was not made out for this lifestyle.

When I went to work, Tom Ford knew straightaway that something was wrong so I told him what had happened. He asked me what arrangements I had made for that night and I told him I would sleep in the same place. He told me to go home, apologize to my parents and leave home. That was not happening. There was no return. I slept in the car for a further three nights.

I couldn't sleep in my car any longer. I was too fat and big to find any comfortable position. I needed to wash and do other things necessary for life. I rented a box room in a house. I lay on my broken single bed and looked up at the lit low voltage light bulb hanging on its own from the ceiling, thinking to myself that this was better than sleeping in a car and I did not deserve any better. I wanted to punish myself. Now this is what you call loneliness. Sleeping in that box room gave me time to think. I could not get any lower in my life. I had now become a tenant, living with at least five other strangers, in the smallest room in a house. I could not see a way out. So I then decided that I needed to plan my end.

I booked my annual leave from work. I had no-one to inform that I was going on leave or to where, only my daughters. I only told them that I needed to get away and think about things. I lay in my little room thinking to myself, more and more "let's do it". Whilst looking for my passport, I found an old pocket size diary and in this book I wrote down a list of important or relevant phone numbers. The first number on the list was H's. For a second, I thought I would phone her. Did she still have my number? I had hers. I thought to myself, what if I rang her and did not like what I heard, how would I feel afterward? I decided not to, then threw the diary in the rusty, dented little tin bin that was in the corner of the room. Consciously I knew that the diary would still be accessible so I took the bin and threw it and its contents into the communal bin outside. I then knew I would not try and get the diary back.

Back in Istanbul

So here I was squeezed into this seat, on a plane on my way to Istanbul. I had lost track of any time, my mobile had run out of battery. I kept on falling in and out of sleep, sedated by all the miniature bottles of brandy. I had lost count of how many I had drunk by then. Before I knew it, the plane was touching down, I was back on land and now my final mission was about to begin. Getting out of the airport was straight forward and rushed, apart from the representative of the border control asking me why I was visiting Turkey. I forcefully swallowed my saliva knowingly that I was lying to him. I was never a good liar. I told him I was just in Istanbul for a holiday. I had visited Turkey on numerous occasions and I was immediately granted a three month visa, with restrictions that I could not work.

Outside the airport, I was instantly welcomed by the dry heat of the season. It was nightfall and getting dark quickly. I got into the next waiting yellow taxi outside the terminal.

I spoke to the driver in Turkish, informing him indirectly that I was not a foreign tourist and was familiar with taxi charges. I told him the name of the hotel, which was in Sirkeci and asked if he knew of it. He said when we get to Sirkeci he would find it. I had chosen this hotel because it was the cheapest and I was vaguely familiar with the area. I sat next to him in the front but just looked out of my door window, throughout the journey, looking out for all the Turkish red and white flags flying in the wind, hanging from buildings, or on poles. I loved Turkey and its flag, maybe it was because it was red. Undoubtedly red was my colour. When we think of love, we always think of red, or was it because my favourite team wore red? Although my parents descended from Cyprus and were Turkish Cypriots, although I was born in Hackney hospital in the East End of London and had lived in England all my life, I had long ago adopted Turkey as being my own. I always felt I was home in Turkey and that Turkey was my country and my identity. So why not die and be buried here?

Sirkeci was about 60km from the airport. The taxi driver seemed to know the area well and this made the journey, thankfully, feel very short. This journey was one of the most unpleasant feelings of loneliness I had ever felt. I found myself sitting in the dark by myself. It was almost 10 o'clock in the evening and I could feel tears running down my cheek gently. I was crying, trying not to attract the driver's attention. Nobody should know what was going on with me. How should anybody know what was happening? Everybody that I knew seemed happier than me, all waiting for tomorrow. But for me, it did not make any difference, I had been there, done that, got the T shirt, got the scars. Before I knew it, it was all gone. Thankfully I was soon outside the hotel well, hostel. Before I went in, I was distracted by a little shop next door. A cross between a souvenir shop and a convenience store, from the outside it looked very small. The front door was single, open and looked wide enough for me to walk in sideways. What attracted me was the half lit, neon light declaring 'We Pierce Ears'. It was the last thing I expected.

Something as little as piercing my ear was a big and long running saga in my life. I had wanted to have an earring in my left ear for as long as I could remember. I never had the courage to tell anyone of this great passion and desire and for over thirty years it was my secret. It was not what men do! It's a sign of being gay! No-one employs men with an earring! Throughout life, I heard these comments again and again. I was too much of a coward to say what I thought or that I wanted one. When I was about forty and felt a bit braver, I would subtlety bring up the conversation, that I liked it, or wanted to have an earring. Father was totally against it, threatening me with disowning, throwing me out of the family home, so to me it was not worth the risk of disrespecting his wishes. My mother was not far from dad on this matter. Anyway, I was now in the middle of Istanbul, outside a 'We Pierce Ears' shop. Thinking, what I was thinking? I walked in, chose an imitation silver encrusted red ruby stud and finally after all that commotion, had my left earlobe pierced. I paid the young lady who had the pleasure with my card. Surely one of the best ten euros I had ever spent. For hours I kept on touching my ear, to see if it was still there. It was one of my proudest personal moments. It was now time to check in.

The Hostel building was positioned in a backstreet, about six floors high. Surrounded by different standards of hotels and restaurants, all were selling similar foods, fish and kebabs, with Efes beer and Sisha being advertised everywhere. I looked up at the building and smiled to myself and thought was this going to be my final home. The hostel proudly called itself Yeni Hotel (New) it may have been a hotel once and it may have been new about fifty years ago. It also did not even look like a hotel. My first impression was as expected. Very rough, it had definitely seen some wear but it was very clean. I was greeted by a man who was obviously proud of the building and trying to impress with his imperfect English. He showed me a copy of my reservation and asked me to pay the bill. I noticed that the man had a visibly disfigured left hand. It was very claw-like and his fingers looked stiff, very knobbly and bony. I refused politely and we smiled at each other, sheepishly, both eloquently acknowledging to each other that we both knew that we were trying to play games with one another. The hotel worker calculatingly, trying to get me to pay a bill for the week that I had booked in advance and had agreed to pay when I left. I was avoiding any sort of payment until I saw what I was getting for my twenty-nine euros per night. Obviously, he did not know my plans. I told him that I did not know exactly how many days I was going to stay and could be staying longer. It seemed that the man was satisfied with that, he was happy that there was a possibility that I was going to be extend my stay. I showed the man respect by calling him Uncle in Turkish and this relaxed the situation. He was a bit suspicious that I was traveling light but laughed out loudly when I told him I had come to Istanbul for shopping. I would be going to the Grand Bazaar as soon as I could to buy clothes. He nodded, telling me that he knew of a cheap chauffeur if I needed a ride. Uncle then gave me my room key, this time with his other hand, which had the same deformity. The key was clearly marked with the number 7 on it, written in white, possibly with correction fluid. The room was based on the first floor and I followed the man up some spiral stairs. The man had an obvious limp but had no problem climbing up the flight of fifteen stairs. The steps were of an irregular shape, wider at one end than the other and I tried to stay at the wider ends, trying to avoid falling. He showed me my room by pointing to the double doors in front of me. The door had a continental 7 written on it with a permanent felt marker. The number had become faint over the years.

Before I could enter the room the man hastily tried to direct me to show me the shower room, which was communal. I wondered to myself how many showers there were on each floor. This room was surprisingly very sparklingly clean, with tiled walls from floor to ceiling. In one corner there was an electric shower heater and in the other corner about six feet up the wall there were about five long nails carefully hammered into the wall, positioned between the tiles. I assumed these were the clothes hangers. I could smell toilet sewage nearby.

The man pointed to the hole in the floor and said this was one of the toilets. I just looked at it and was reminded of my granddad's house in Lefkara, Cyprus when I visited it in the mid 1960's when I was about five years old. It was just a hole in the floor. The man looked at me, noticing my change in emotion and laughed out loud. Before I could say anything, he led me to another toilet which was the conventional style of toilet. I could tell from the sarcasm of the man that he could not imagine me crouching and doing a number two in the hole in the floor. He was so right. I opened my room, only one of the double doors opened. Again I was pleasantly surprised as it was very clean and spacious. One single bed, covered with a sheet and a very thin blanket, one pillow without a case and an old mahogany-style heavy wardrobe in the corner. This was open inside, showing one wire hanger. I could hear everything going on outside, cars passing, people eating and talking in the restaurant down below. Closing the window did not cut out much of the sound, but it reduced the noise which did not bother me. There was no towel and I presumed no room service either. This hotel room was definitely Gideon free. I decided not to shower. I switched off the light, the room lit only by the 'EFES' neon light flashing somewhere outside. I slept to escape from reality.

Sleeping was the only thing that would make me forgot the pains that I was feeling. I just lay on the bed, thinking and reflecting to myself. I was not expecting this but I could not see any way out. I will always be in this situation. Things in my life were not going to change. I could not see any turning point or change in my life, I had let my loved ones down and I had discarded their love. I had finally lost the woman I loved. I was crippled by debt, gambling had caused me to become blacklisted by more than one bank and credit card company debt collection agencies were also chasing me. My debts were too high. Where did it all go wrong? I was always a freedom fighter, fighting the corner of the underdog. I had run away to be alone, now I was fighting myself.

My first night's sleep was broken by the local Imam calling the locals to prayer. It seemed that I had only slept for a few minutes but had been asleep far longer. The narcotic effect of the brandy in my bloodstream and jet lag was a great anesthetic. I stayed lying on my single bed, touching my earlobe to feel if the earring was still there. I could feel the heat from outside. It was already getting hot. I was uncovered as there was no need for covers. I did not expect Istanbul to be so warm in September. I just looked up at the ceiling. I noticed I was doing a lot of this lately, studying light bulbs. This was one of those environmentally friendly spiral light bulbs, dangling by its long yellow discoloured cord, hanging centrally from the ceiling. Emotional tiredness was just so hard to handle that any physical sleep could not take it away. I thought resting my heart is the only way to get through this tiredness. Anxiety and depression often kept me lying awake at night. I looked out of the window. I could see a road sweeper leaning on his broom, the broom handle was taller than the sweeper and I could not tell if this was because he was short or that the handle was just longer. He looked like he was enjoying a cigarette, puffing at it as if it was his last, sucking out all the nicotine, and then breathing out the smoke as if it was sweet, satisfying steam. I looked at him and thought to myself that his life looked better than mine. I continued thinking to myself - I bet he had a loving wife at home! I was then distracted by a cat that was eating something out of a leaking rubbish bag. I even envied the cat and its freedom from any problems. Then I thought to myself, I will go and get some breakfast too. No need to worry about dieting, I could now eat whatever I wanted, without worrying about the calories.

It was the first day of the new beginning. I needed money, so I needed to withdraw cash from somewhere. ATMs were all over the place, so that was no issue. I had not thought of when I was going to kill myself or how, so that was next. Funny as it was, after forty years of depression and turmoil I felt the happiest I had ever been. I now had no fears, I was free and I accepted that I had messed up, had my chances and wasted them. It was time to say goodbye. Ironically as that may sound, it was time to move on.

I felt more visible in Turkey. In fact, I noticed that I had stopped hiding. I felt for the first time fearless, enlightened more than I had ever been in my life as this big obese man. As I began what would become my daily walk to the rocks on the Bosporus, however, I still noticed the pairs of eyes that stared at me. It felt as if someone was stamping on my very existence. As I stood alone waiting to cross the crazy busy streets in Sirkeci, cars, lorries, dust-covered buses and trams beeped loudly, all full of people. As pedestrians passed me on my left and right, I desperately tried to avoid any eye contact and nervously glanced at the buildings, as if I was lost. But I felt their eyes burning through me like lasers. I would find myself questioning and wondering what is so different about me. Was I that strange?

I walked about two hundred metres, very slowly, as I was very unfit. I crossed a busy major road and could see the flowing waters of the Bosporus and on the banks, there were little kiosks all selling different things, some trading newspapers, sweets, cigarettes, others sandwiches.

My attention was attracted to a street seller who was sitting on an old three-legged splintered wooden stool, one the legs of the stool shorter than the other two and the man looked like he was going to fall off it. The man looked about my height although he was sitting down but he was very big, a lot bigger than I was, maybe that was what attracted me to him. Both his thighs were wrapped tightly by white bandages, one leg whiter than the other. He was selling fresh simit bread. These were like New York pretzels covered in sesame seeds. I kept on staring and he soon clocked me as a potential customer and waved his hand for me to approach him. I obliged and we exchanged a few words. I bought one for 1 lira and started to take bites of it whilst walking away. Three hundred metres further I could now see the Bosporus approach and the ferries in it became clearer. The streets were now filling up with people on their way to work and cars were slowing down because of the accumulation of traffic. The decibels in the atmosphere were increasing by the minute, the air was slowly getting polluted with exhaust fumes and with sounds of cars hooting, boats horns and ringing bells of the trams. Street sellers were all trying to over-shout each other selling simits, freshly filled rolls and of course Turkish Tea. Others were peeling and putting fresh corn on the cob into boiling water for later sales. Welcome to Istanbul, my friend! I said to myself. I bought myself a tea and put the sugar offered into it. It was all served in a throw-away see-through cup and watching the sugar lumps dissolve in the bottom of the cup was nice. For years I had always drunk my tea unsweetened or with saccharine, trying to save on my calorie intake, but the taste of real sugar was truly delicious. Again I thought to myself, so what if I was going to put on more weight, I'll be dead in the next few days.

I walked in the direction towards the Bosphorus where I could see a bridge. My thoughts at first were that this could be it, how I could do it. Find a suitable place and jump off, simple. I walked as near to it as possible. The bridge was about fifteen hundred meters long. I tried to look at the best place I could jump down from. I was not going to do it at this present time but when I was ready. Where was the best way and could I access it? I could not see a suitable opening or place where I thought I could get to the bridge without making a scene or people noticing me. The last thing I wanted was to mess this up also. I could never go through the humiliation of getting this wrong too, by surviving or being stopped. So this was my first idea of how to do it.

Whilst walking back I popped into one of the internet cafes nearby. I thought I would do some research on this. I was curious about the number of suicides that had taken place on the bridges of Istanbul and found that during its first years of opening, pedestrians could walk across the bridge and where there were elevators inside the legs of the bridge, these were open to the public. However, after many suicides, it was no longer open to pedestrians. Clearly, others had the same idea as me and both bridges on the Bosphorus were closed. I wanted this mission of mine to be perfect. I chose Turkey to be my place of suicide because I wanted to be buried there. I never ever wanted to be buried in the Muslim tradition or as a Muslim and knew this was a big contradiction but whenever I discussed my death and funeral wishes with family, they said I was mad, and I knew they would not follow my final wishes on how I wanted my funeral. I did not want to be buried in the customary cemetery where people I had known were buried. Coincidently this cemetery was in the town in which I had spent the majority of my life and it was in the road that I had worked in for the last seven years. I wanted my coffin draped with the red and white of the Turkish flag. At least if I did die in Turkey without anyone knowing, I had control of my destiny. I felt my family did not show me any respect when I spoke about my ideal funeral when I was alive so why would they respect me now, when I was dead. I planned leaving a note and instructions on myself, as to how I wanted my burial to be carried out quickly without their influence. So jumping from a bridge over the Bosphorus was ruled out quickly. I knew that I wanted to die instantly and did not want to get it wrong and be saved, or worse not die and become disabled. I could not go back to the UK. I did not want to be a burden to anyone.

I then considered my second option, which was to shoot myself, but where could I get a gun? Whilst walking back to the hotel, thinking about what, where and how, I was being distracted by growing pains in my right leg and sore feet. All of a sudden I heard a loud, long screech and bells sounding. I could feel on my back the wind that had been broken by the tram. The screech sounded like a lifetime. I did not know it at the time, but I had stepped in front of a coming tram. All I remembered for that split second was looking at the tram driver who was making rude angry hand signs towards me. I was not ruffled at all but I could see the faces of others who witnessed my close encounter. A particular lady covered in Shailer had her hand over her open mouth and her eyes were open wide, looking at me with shock. I think the tram missed me by a literally a whisker. I was more embarrassed than scared. I thought to myself, another second earlier and my mission would have been completed. Killed by a speeding tram? How convenient would that have been? Well, I walked away thinking to myself that was now maybe a third option? Or maybe God did not want me dead?

Immediately opposite my hotel was a very poorly furnished fish restaurant. I had planned that I would make this my usual eating place and would try to have my evening meal on a customary basis. I thought it would be the place to start to familiarise myself with the area, getting to know the locals, maybe this was where I could get information on where I could get the gun. It was getting dark. I could now feel both my legs getting tired and my feet were blistering. I had not worn socks that morning because I had not packed any and did not think that I would have done so much walking.

Before I even walked into the restaurant, I was approached by this man in a suit holding the roughest and obviously much-used menu covered with fingerprints. He immediately pointed out what the restaurant had on the menu, showing me photos of dead fish on a plate. He kept on saying "fish and chips, fish and chips?" in English with an accent, as he pointed to a table, pulling out a chair at the same time. When I nodded and walked into the restaurant, the man became excited and rushed over. I told him that I would prefer to sit inside and the waiter was pleasantly shocked when I spoke to him in his language. "You speak Turkish well," he said. I just nodded. The food was good and cheap, sea bass and chips was the closest to fish and chips I had enjoyed for ages. I tried to keep myself to myself. Another young waiter who bought me my food had obviously been told that I could speak Turkish. He seemed more interested in me and asked me questions about myself. I tried to avoid giving him straight answers at first but he was insistent and conversation developed. I could see my hostel from where I was sitting. I could see straight through to the reception area. Sitting in the doorway of the hotel was Uncle. I thought to myself, this man worked long hours. After my meal and of course the usual complimentary Turkish tea, I went over to him. It was a warm night and I was not ready for bed. I sat next to him and we started to speak. I found out that night the man's name was Ersen but everyone knew him as Billy G. He said he was named Billy G by an American tourist about thirty years ago and it had stuck with him ever since. He told me that he owned the hotel. It was his home.

Going to bed early at night made it easy for me to get up very early the next day. No amount of sleep in the world could cure the tiredness I felt. I was used to hearing the seagulls singing above, living in Hastings when in England, but the cockerels crowing from yonder and the Imam calling the locals for prayer was a different atmosphere. I tried to listen to the sound coming from the mosque asking myself if that was a recording or a real Imam. I could not tell. These sounds always made the morning and became my alarm call. It soon became a ritual that every morning for my breakfast I bought myself a simit from the same seller and quickly started to talk to him more and more. It was not long before I started opening up him. Maybe it was because he looked so much like a fatter version of my dad.

VEDAT

I found out that the man who sold the simits was a man called Vedat. I started to talk to him, exchanging a few words each time, saying more and more. We soon became friends and after about the third day and my sixth simit he started telling me things about himself in a boastful way and promoting his stall. He slowly started talking about other things like what we had in common, firstly talking and letting me know how patriotic he was. He loved the fact that he was born a Turk. He cherished his country. He respected the Army and its significance of protecting his Motherland. He treasured the sights of the flying Turkish red and white flags proudly displayed everywhere. Vedat was very familiar with the area. He taught me some facts about Sirkeci.

The name Sirkeci meant "vinegar-maker". This district between Sultan Ahmet and Eminönü, very near the Galata Bridge and the Golden Horn, was known not for its vinegar but for its transportation. The shipping and carrying of people to two continents is what makes Sirkeci what it was. Vedat proudly told me how The Ottoman Sultan built Istanbul's European railroad terminus, Sirkeci Gar, on the Golden Horn right beneath the walls of Topkapi Palace. He recommended that I should take a short tram ride from Sultan Ahmet, or even walk to the Eminönü ferry docks and he advised me to spend time looking at the buildings around The Spice Bazaar, rather than in it. Some people even believed that the biblical event of Noah's flood occurred in this area. He told me about the Sirkeci Station and said it was the terminus for many trains to and from Europe.

He explained that life was like a train destination; if you jump off you stand still but the train will continue to go on. It will not be held up. Sometimes a train stops where you do not expect it to stop and occasionally it may go to places you do not know. We soon started talking about ourselves. I told him about my love for Turkey and respect of the Turkish flag also and that even I was, to a certain extent, mystified and confused to as why that was the case. Although I was born and spent almost all my life in England I had never felt at home. Whenever I was in Istanbul, I felt at home. Vedat told me that inside all of us, there was a desire for a home, everybody needs a home. He said he didn't understand the British culture as they make shorts and pants out of their flag, and wear them. He felt that was disrespectful.

Vedat soon started to explain to me how he had found himself where he was, selling simits during the day and in the evenings selling roasted chestnuts till late into the night. He told me that he had been trading in the same area for over sixty years. His day would start at 5am when his wife and he would bake the first batch of simits, he would load up his barrow and be at his pitch by 7am selling till 10pm in the winter, later in the summer months, seven days a week. His wife would be on alert to deliver a fresh lot of loaves of bread when he was running short. He would swap his barrow for a transportable purpose-made mini-barbecue where he would keep himself warm and roast the chestnuts or sometimes fresh sweet corn on the cob. Vedat more and more reminded me of my father and I soon fell in love with him.

On about the fifth day Vedat had placed beside him a second wooden stool. When he saw me approaching he called out to me, "Hey cuddly, look what I have got for you! I know you cannot stand up for long" and pointed down to the stool. I was unbelievably thrilled by his gesture at the time and was surprised within myself that this small deed had made me so happy. I used to tell him bits of my life story and he would tell me parts of his. Every now and then he would put his hand in the bread cabinet and pull out a simit and break it into two, giving me one half of a wedge of cheese spread and some slices of tomato, all served on a serviette. He would eat the other half himself.

Vedat was originally from Izmir and was orphaned very young. He went to live with his auntie, the alternative at the time being an orphanage three hundred miles away. Vedat soon ran away from his auntie when he was six years old. He told me how his auntie's second husband used to beat him for any purpose daily, sometimes for no reason. Eventually he made his way from Izmir to Istanbul. This journey took about two years, during which time he had lived rough on the streets, eventually making it to Sirkeci. When he arrived in Istanbul, another simit seller kind of adopted him. This is where he learned about baking and selling. Vedat called his adopted father Usta (governor). Usta was getting old and tired and he eventually left him in charge of the pitch and the trolley to carry on the business. The old man would bake the bread for him and Vedat would sell them. He was only eleven or twelve at the time.

Every morning a young school girl with her mother would pass the stall and buy a simit from him. Vedat soon fell in love with the little school girl, but could not say anything because he was afraid of scaring her off. He pointed out that "this was Turkey, it's not right to say things like 'I like you' it was not appropriate". Anyway he felt that she was too classy for him; even though they were the same age, they were so different. She was a child, who had two parents, she was going to school and getting an education. He had no mum or dad and was already a man working to survive. He was just a street seller. It was not long before the girl started going to school on her own but she continued to buy simits from him every morning on school days. He found out that her name was Gurnas. They soon became good friends. Vedat wanted to talk to her so much and he wanted to take her out on a date. He had fantasies of them both having a picnic together. He did not even have the courage to talk to her. He could not even ask her, he kept on thinking that she was too superior for him. He would take her money and just smile when he saw her. This went on for years. Gurnas became a woman but he remained a simit seller in love. Vedat knew if he did not let his princess know of his feelings, he was going to lose her. So on December 2nd (he would never forget that date), on a very cold icy day, he got the courage and told Gurnas how he felt and how long he had had these feelings. He knew that he had to say something to her so that his ordeal would end one way or another. Then came the shock of his life. Gurnas told him that she did not even like simits.

Vedat got scared for a few seconds. She told him that she only bought a simit in the morning so as to see him and talk to him. She told him that she knew that he was shy. She asked him what had taken him so long, and that she was beginning to give up. She would usually throw the simit away that she had bought into the Bosporus for the seagulls, always asking God to forgive her for treating bread with so much disrespect. Vedat's face shone with a smile as he continued to tell me his story. Vedat told me when he heard how Gurnas had felt about him, it was as if he had won the lottery, it was the greatest day of his life. They were now both sixteen and it was the start of a secret affair. Vedat would talk to me about Gurnas with a smile, his eyes would sparkle, and his mouth would salivate. He loved her then and he loved her more now. He would not use her name often when talking about her but he would call her his 'dream' or his 'life'. Since that day there had never ever been a day when they never saw each other. Even when he had to do his army conscription, he was based in Istanbul, to be close to her.

Every day when we met up, Vedat would tell me more about the love story and how his life progressed. It was not long after the couple started seeing each other that Vedat was lonely and felt that he wanted the relationship to move faster. Gurnas was not going to have any of it. She demanded marriage or nothing. Vedat knew that this would be the biggest challenge of his life so far - hitchhiking from Izmir to Istanbul was easy compared with this. He felt that he had nothing and she could have everything. He asked himself, what could he offer her? If he went to her father, he would have been humiliated; he was an orphan, a street seller. Gurnas thought differently and she demanded that Vedat should prove that he was an honourable man and go to see her father. Vedat decided to ask the 'governor' to be his representative, knowing that the old man by now was very frail and could hardly walk without walking sticks. The old man was the closest thing he had to a father. So one day, he got the courage; not because he was brave but he felt he had to move fast as he thought the old man may not have long too live and who else would represent him? The old man agreed to represent him, as long as Vedat understood and knew what he was getting into. The old man told him that "Marriage was like a locked room, no doors, and no windows – no way out! You have to work it out." Vedat booked a taxi. Actually it was a friend he had met on the streets, had a bath and the three musketeers as he called himself and his friends went to Gurnas's house. There was one more problem. Who was going to run the business when he was away? Gurnas, of course.

To his own surprise, Vedat was not nervous in meeting his potential in-laws, he knew Gurnas's mother vaguely. The request for his love's hand in marriage was carried out with respect and tradition. The Governor started the conversation, talking about why they were there and that Vedat was his son. He gave his adopted son a glowing report. Vedat's potential father-in-law said that he was not proud and that he was a man of God. He had listened and accepted that his daughter was in love, he believed that it would have been against God's will to separate a couple who were obviously one. All he asked was that his future son-in-law would become a son who would treat his daughter as well as he did. He looked at Vedat and asked him if he could look after his daughter. Vedat just nodded, humbly. His father-in-law then told everyone that he saw no reason to bless them both. Vedat was confident and was sure that he would look after his princess for all his life. Vedat kissed his new father-in-law's hand and as far as Vedat knew, he was now a husband to the women he loved. From that day till now Vedat and Gurnas had been together.

Vedat and his wife agreed to look and take care of the governor as long as he lived in exchange for living in his humble home. Gurnas became the new baker and the head of the household. Before long Gurnas found out that she was pregnant and gave birth to a son who Vedat cheekily described as a lazy good-for-nothing son. Apparently he was Gurnas's pride and joy and she spent all her money on him from the day he was born. Vedat then said amusingly, that he only kissed his wife once after that and she was pregnant again and she gave birth to his beautiful baby girl. I could see from the sparkle in his eye that she was his favourite. He more than once reminded me that she was now a successful surgeon practicing in a hospital in Ankara. She had also given him four lovely granddaughters. Vedat was swollen with pride in what he had achieved from selling bread, owning his own business, having a wonderful wife and raising two children whom he had financed and educated to university level. He was king of his fate, in charge of his destiny. He told me when he got married everything he got was bought from money he made by selling simits. Every week they would buy something for the house. One week they would buy a fork, the next a knife. For weeks he and his wife would eat with the same spoon, waiting for the other to finish what they were eating. Then when they had a set, they would buy a cup. This carried on for years. The governor was a very minimal man who lived a modest life and he had given everything he had to Vedat and had no more. The governor lived for another six years with them before he passed away.

Vedat continued to tell me that his son also went to university but he never did anything with his studies apart from meeting and marrying his wife when he was supposed to be studying. When I asked what his son was doing now, he just quickly spoke under his breath and said, "Spending his father-in-law's money". Vedat always laughed when he was talking about his children, especially about his son. He thought his son was fixated with his wife. Vedat did though have a sense of humour, especially when he was talking about his eldest child; he obviously loved him greatly. He never denied his favoritism towards his daughter and her successful achievements as a doctor. He often said that his son was not the son he would have chosen. It was quite odd to me that he would he wished that his son worked at the local supermarket as a cashier. I did not believe him because whenever he criticized his son, he would glow with a smile on his face. He told me how his son had become infatuated with a girl that he had met whilst at university. The girl worked part-time in the college library and she became his fascination and then he became a yes man. She took over. Vedat said that he lost his son the day he met that girl. He described her as his daughter too and loved her like his own and said that she was an honorable girl - it was his son that he felt let down by. I never did understand why. Maybe Vedat expected his son to stay by his side. I am sure he was not expecting his son to take over the family business. I think Vedat was heartbroken that his children and now also his grandchildren were not around him and lived a distance away.

Vedat was very proud of what he had achieved in his life and often conceitedly described himself as an honest street rascal. His antics were most of the time very funny and watching him working, listening to him speaking to passers-by, he could spot a tourist from a mile, using all the different languages that he had learned from living on the streets. I often wondered if he spoke to them in the way he spoke English. He was not very good. He used the same chat up lines to any new face he met and if he saw the customers again, he never forgot the face or where the tourist had come from. Once he had 'clocked' that someone was interested in his offerings, he would have his paper bag opened, instantly pick whatever he was selling from his display and give it to the customer, who rarely said no. He would start the conversation, asking them if they were Swedish, this was the trigger point for the customer to say no, they were from somewhere else. I do not know why he chose Swedish. I never heard anyone say they were from Sweden. In between the questions, he would ask the customer if they wanted cheese with their simit. The cheese was just a triangular soft cheese wrapped in foil. Wanting cheese would now double the price and the simit became a sandwich. Then it was, you want ah cola? With this script Vedat would run his business. He was very good at it, loved what he was doing and I never heard anyone say anything bad about Vedat. In fact, I certainly did not meet anyone who knew Vedat, who did not love him. Whoever passed him during the day who knew him would salute or shout out greetings.

People started getting used to seeing me daily and quickly started saluting me too. Vedat was very experienced in life and he did not hesitate to pass on these life skills, but he was honest about what he said to me. These conversations with Vedat were spread out and as I told him bits of my life, I talked to him mostly about my disastrous love affair with H and my business ventures.

Vedat then told me that when I spoke to him he sensed that I was a broken man, from the day he met me. He frequently told me that life was never over until you die and that I was clever enough to start again and that life was for living. He told me if I was not clever enough I should start eating 'Chicken Legs'. I looked at him bewildered and asked, "What's all this got to do with chicken legs?" Vedat burst out in laughter and continued to tell me this story.

"Abdul and Safiye recently got married and rented a flat above a food store. Abdul would go to work every day and Safiye would go downstairs to shop. She became chatty with the food store owner Mr. Karim. One day Safiye noticed that Mr. Karim had bought himself a new car. She congratulated him on his new purchase, commenting that her husband was a hard worker and couldn't afford a car or their own home. How could Mr. Karim afford such a luxury? He replied that you must use your brain and be clever. Safiye asked Mr. Karim how he got so clever. Mr. Karim replied "I eat lots of chicken legs". She asked, "Chicken legs?" He told her if you eat chicken legs every day you will get clever. So Safiye decided to feed her husband chicken legs. That evening she cooked her husband chicken legs for his supper. The next day in his lunch box Abdul found for his lunch - chicken legs. Abdul was too nice to complain at first. Safiye continued serving chicken legs to her husband for the next five days for lunch and supper. Abdul eventually got the courage to question his wife's cooking. He asked her why they were eating chicken legs every day. Safiye told him that Mr. Karim told her that chicken legs were brain food. If you want to get clever you must eat lots of them. Abdul asked his wife how much she was paying for the chicken legs. She said she paid £1 each for them. Abdul then explained to his wife that two chicken legs would cost her £2. He continued to tell her that she could buy a whole chicken for £3. When Safiye went downstairs to the shop the next day Mr. Karim started to wrap the usual order of chicken legs. Safiye immediately stopped Mr. Karim and told him she was not going to buy two chicken legs for £2 when she could get a whole chicken for £3. Mr. Karim replied, "You see, you and your husband have only been eating chicken legs for five days and you are both now cleverer!"

The story made me laugh but also had a meaningful thought to it. I smiled and walked off. I was too much of a coward to tell him of my inner thoughts and why I had really come to Turkey. He was too much of a romantic to deserve my baggage or my 'I'm a victim' story. Vedat's stories would always end by him saying "God was good!" Although Vedat acknowledged the existence of a God, he was disappointed that he was not a more Godly person and felt that God was not happy with him and how he had conducted his life, but felt that God understood that everything he had done in his life was about survival. Vedat had often said that he was unlucky in life but was in fact very blessed. He admitted throughout his life having a best friend relationship with God. God was, in fact, his only friend. Since he could remember from the age of six when he lived and slept on the streets, he felt the spiritual presence over him protecting him and providing for him. Later on, he met the governor who took him under his wing, providing him with shelter and feeding him. Vedat believed that the Governor was an Angel sent to him from above. I admired this about Vedat, being so meek, and very generous. These were two great qualities that I well-liked and admired in a person.

Vedat was a family man through and through and he loved family passionately. I could tell that he was not happy with me when I told him of the way I had met H and how the relationship had developed. He told me that in the past he had similar offers, especially living on the streets and he had come in contact with many women that he fancied and liked. He would put on his serious face and say, "I was not always this old, fat man, you know!" He told me a story of a situation whilst his wife was in hospital recovering after giving birth to having their first child. The neighbor came around to ask about the baby and his wife. She brought with her a saucepan of hot soup. Whilst talking he did not know how the conversation had got onto the subject but the neighbor had recently come out of hospital herself, where she had a lump removed from one of her breasts. The lady insisted on showing him the scar. Before he could say anything the lady removed her top showing off her bare breasts. She then asked him if he wanted to feel where the lump was. The lady was surprised and disappointed when, like a gentleman, he refused, just saying "no thank you". The woman replied by saying to him, "You do respect the sanctity of your marriage, don't you?" He nodded and told her that he was flattered by her offer but no thank you. Vedat commented, looking into my eyes; "That while his wife was recovering, from giving birth to a baby for him, how he could be tempted by another woman's flesh and disrespect her? You know that tingling feeling you get when you like someone? Well, that's common sense leaving your head!" I could not stop myself but laugh at what he said.

He continued to tell me that he believed that a man has to be groomed to be a husband. Husbands and wives have different functions in life, each should know what their roles are. There should be no mistake in the home who the mummy and daddy are, your children must know this. A husband should be a protector, like a roof that covers a house. Your wife should feel secure and safe spiritually, physically and emotionally. A husband must be a provider, not necessarily of just money. Vedat told me that as a husband you must lead by example. Love was not enough, there was nothing wrong with being in love, but a husband had to be committed to love even after marriage. He told me "He who loves his wife, loves himself" When you get married you build a friendship. You must find out what your wife likes. Communication is important and you should find joint common interests. It is important that you value your wife like you would respect your female boss. Vedat then made me laugh; he asked me if I would pass wind in front of my boss, especially if she was a woman. I laughed but knew he was right and where he was coming from. Another great opinion that Vedat had about marriage was that one should not have high expectations of your wife. I looked at him bewildered. He then told me in a harsh voice, screwing up his face "She's not your mother!" I then nodded as in agreement. Vedat then amazed me even more. He told me that one important thing that keeps a marriage alive was that one has to keep dating. Again I was now getting more muddled but he continued saying you should not stop dating your wife. He explained before you get married, you take care with yourself, you keep yourself fit, you wash, smell nice. You watch what you say, you behave yourself. One should not stop because you are now married. Again Vedat raised his voice and started

157

pointing his finger at me, telling me that when married you should never forget special occasions, keep on saying nice words to her, keep on buying her flowers. He told me if you want a strong marriage, be kind to your wife.

My experience with marriages was not a good one. Deep down though, however much I have tried to justify my behavior and the reasons for leaving my first wife, I then began to accept it was immoral being an adulterer. I tried to tell Vedat how life was in the last few years with H and how she told me that she loved me but was not in love with me anymore. I explained to Vedat how I would ignore what she was saying and carried on hanging on to whatever emotion H would give to me. Vedat told me to focus on myself and not on her anymore. He told me that the issue was not what was behind me, rather it is what was in front of me. He told me how I should stop worshiping the past and to be aware of the peril of familiarity. Familiarity breeds contempt. I had imprisoned myself, because of hatred. I had no reason to hate, but he explained how I had built this wall around my heart and no longer was letting anyone in, incarcerated by unforgiveness. He told me how he was sure that H had moved on, so I should let go, but I was shackled in my own heart because I had surrounded myself with this unforgiveness. I should learn to discipline my flesh and take control. He continued to tell me that there were things in me which bothered me and if I wanted to live, I should let go. For others to love and respect me, I have to love and respect myself. To do this, I may need to make practical, significant changes in my life. Vedat then started to tell me of another one of his stories that he had read.

"In about the 15th century, an explorer, Hernando Cortez, was planning to build a colony near the Bay of Vera-Cruz in Mexico. When he told the Spanish Governor of his plans, the

Governor got excited and gave him eleven ships and seven hundred men to fulfill the expedition. As soon as they landed and unloaded the ships, he set the ships on fire and they sunk. Cortez understood the dangers of keeping your options open. He knew that there were going to be in difficult times and if the soldiers knew their ships were on standby, they did not have to be there. They would not fight as well. Cortez removed their options".

No plan B or options, you will fight your way out. We know most things in life and we know what to do. Of course there are things in life that we don't know. Keeping hold of choices affects your vision and when you have too many options there is a danger of making the wrong decisions. I gave up on my first marriage when I had an option. I held onto the option of running to my father's house whenever a problem arose. Vedat told me that one of the most important things I should have done when H told me that she did not love me anymore was to take a step back – but I chose to move closer. I could see in Vedat's face he was disappointed in me, he told me that I should now look and find my self-identity and that I had lost respect for myself. He continued saying "The comeback was always stronger than the setback". I should use this holiday in Istanbul to figure out who I was. To let go of someone I loved, I should start to write down my dreams, a sort of 'bucket list' and take specific action steps towards achieving them. No one can stop me from reaching my destiny than myself. He said that if one has no goals you will have nothing to aim for, so you will hit nothing. He told me that I should give myself space to heal and breathe. Maybe this meant me losing a few pounds in weight, or spending more time with other people I respect or respected me. Vedat told me that I had invested in this relationship for years and now, I needed to look at it objectively, with my mind and gut, not my heart. Was this the relationship I wanted for myself? No matter how painful it is if you are in love, you always hope for better things to happen even though it would be easier just to give up.

Vedat asked me, before I had met H, would I have wanted my best friend to be in this relationship? Did H willingly meet my needs and respect my wishes? Did I do the same for her? He asked me to be honest with myself and if I had to do it all over again, ask myself if I would choose H again as my partner. He continued to tell me how God was stripping away all the rot in my life, which I no longer needed, to make room for something more wonderful than I could ever imagine. Vedat told me when someone gets married and things do not go as expected, things do not work out, one should not look at the easiest way out, just because you are experiencing turbulence. When there is turbulence in a plane you cannot open the window and jump out, you must keep your seat belt on and sit tight.

These thoughts of wisdom made me really think about the past and help me look at my relationships. Vedat suggested that I should start looking at new activities to put into my life plan, maybe a trip to go somewhere, a place that I wanted to see. He asked why I did not go to Israel, as I always wanted to go to Israel. For some reason he remembered that I had told him this before, on an occasion when he was talking to a couple of tourists visiting Sisli, who were from Jerusalem. He also told me to join that scuba diving club that I wanted to. This was another one of my fantasies that I had mentioned to Vedat (or did I?) Go and find a new place to live. It doesn't matter what the new actions are, really what is important was that I should find new, interesting things to do with my life, rather than carry on being obsessed with my ex-wife, girlfriend, lover or whatever I called her. Vedat put on his sarcastic tone into his voice and started flapping his index fingers on both hands, trying to act as if that he was a university academic. You then can start to practice replacing this 'obsession' with something new and interesting. He also told me that I should let go of the child that was inside of me, 'the clown' as I call him. He told me that as a child, I was expected to grow up too early, I was given too much responsibility as a child. It was unfortunate that I was left to my own devices to grow up and make my own decisions, many of which were wrong decisions. At an early age I was expected to translate for my mother, go to the doctors on my own, and help run the family business. He told me how unconsciously I had held onto the childhood that was taken away from me and it was time to let go. I was just amazed at how much wisdom Vedat had. He knew me so well.

Vedat was a man who could make things obvious to me and was able to open my heart in a way no other person or counselor had ever been able to do. He made me realize that I was battling with a lot of confusion and that this passion had replaced the truth and that I was engrossed in drama, enslaved in rogue emotions. High drama seemed to be the norm and the truth was no longer an issue; I had let emotions distort the truth for far too long. I had been living life, drama after drama for the past twenty years. Addicted to emotions, I was so involved in self-flagellation that I was damaging myself beyond repair. All these detrimental emotions had got in the way of my relationships. Vedat explained to me that I could not have love as long as I was holding onto hate. He told me some home truths that I was too blind to see. Vedat told me that my crisis was of my own making; I had removed myself from the place I should be and from people I should be with. I was hiding; I did not want to be seen, as I had failed. It was all about my image. I did not know who I was. My behavior in the past had made me forget that I was a son, husband or most importantly a father. I hated the fact I was expected to be accountable. I loved being the victim. I had been neglecting responsibility. It was easier to react when things went wrong than act on things that went right.

I started to realize how angry I was in life. I started to ask myself how does one process life's tragedies, get over the betrayals, the agonies of life and manage the pain. These emotions had become addictive, making me vulnerable. Vedat also told me that one makes life's choices that make you answerable in the future. He told me to stop hiding in my mind, as this mind was taking me places I did not want to be. He continued to explain to me about the dangers of living in a fantasy. It was dangerous when it takes over one's mind, one loses touch with reality. One should not allow one's fantasy becoming addictive; having so many dreams becomes the means of survival.

He explained that we all have a purpose for this life. He told me that my dreams had become my idols, but did ever I ask myself who cared? Nobody cares what dreams one has. He told me that I should consider my destiny, ask myself what did I want in life? Money, fame, recognition, I had to make choices. He reminded me that I knew that I was not living how I should be. He told me that the world would chew me up and spit me out. He told me that I should think about my actions. If I did not change, at the end I would have nothing. Money should not make you, you should make money. Vedat had given me the vision to recognize that I needed to step out of my misery, as he explained to me that "Wherever you start off in life, you don't have to finish!" I was living in bitterness and desired to surrender the bitterness I was holding onto. I had to release myself from the chains that were holding me back. He told me how desire could ruin a life and that these cravings were a powerful force. He explained how my need had got me to Istanbul. One can long to be great and this aspiration can be a very potent lust, for things we do not need. Vedat continued to tell me how one's craving for things that you know are illicit, illegal or just bad, draw us away from the truth, whilst mental fights and wars come from desires of pleasure. I started to think to myself; what was the truth? Throughout life, I struggled in deciding what was right. I did not resist in doing the wrong things such as gambling, walking away from my marriages, leaving my kids behind, but struggled with being a good person, like the good son, husband, and father. My immaturity made me lose control of my life. I had my life sucked out of me. Vedat had acknowledged that I was broken hearted, my emotions shattered and he kept on telling me that if I wanted any kind of healing I had to acknowledge whatever I did wrong in the past. At some point, I had to realize that some people can stay in your heart but not in your life.

Some people were just meant to be a life lesson, they will just be a bit-part in your life, but the memories will always be in your heart. Although some people may leave our lives, this is not a reason to feel sad. People come and go from our lives for a reason. He continued to explain, "The broken will always be able to love again and better next time because once you've been in the dark, and you learn to appreciate everything that gleams."

I needed to stop thinking that I was to blame and start to deal with those things that hurt me. He assured me that I would not feel this way forever. I knew he was so right, it was so true!

I questioned myself, was Vedat in my head, was he my mind?

ISA

I had been in Istanbul now for four days and had discovered a fish market near to Sultan Ahmet on the Bosphorus. The market was fascinating; it not only sold fresh fish but also fruit and vegetables. Behind the market were many fish restaurants, it was truly a fish lovers' paradise. The restaurants catered for all; you could get a fish sandwich and all cooked in front of you whilst you waited, or go into one of the richer, decorated restaurants and eat a five-course meal. I would just walk around the market, spellbound by the different varieties of fish, all lying on a slab of white marble, every now and then being cooled down by the fishmonger just spraying cold water over them. I later found out that the market was more than five miles from my hotel. I could not believe I had walked five miles there and back on numerous occasions over the day.

The walk was along the coastline of the Bosphorus, from the port of Sirkeci, and this coastline was shared by hundreds of fishermen, the majority of them with rods. From the first sign of daylight you could witness people of all ages using all kinds of fishing equipment. I was no expert but some of it was primitive. The fishermen would find their usual spot setting up busily with their rods, using bread as bait. For these fishermen, the turquoise waters of the Bosphorus were their workplace and extracting a living from the depths of the sea was their way of life. For one certain man, this was not just his place of work but his home.

Isa was a military veteran who had been fishing and supporting himself off of the Bosphorus' since the early 1980s. I first noticed him sitting on an armchair-shaped seat made up and cleverly put together of grey phosphorous heavy rocks. Isa was sitting with a group of about six other men, drinking what looked like Raki and smoking a cigarette made from hand-rolled tobacco. By his side was a small white dog with brown patches. I found out later he was a she and was an almost perfect King Charles Cavalier. I stopped and just watched. The noise coming from them was so joyful and happy. I could smell fish being grilled but could not see anything being cooked, only seeing glimmers of smoke and smelling burning of fish oils. The old man looked at my direction and then the rest of the group looked over to me. They all waved at me and made hand gestures to join them. I returned the hand signals back politely saying no and pointing to the rocks, trying to indicate I could not, it looked too difficult and dangerous. Most of the group was topless and bronzed, suntanned from the past summer. I carried on walking and on my return passed the rock-shaped armchair. This time the group had left but the old man was sitting on his own, with his half glass of Raki. When he saw me looking again he invited me to his side.

I looked at the rocks that lead to him, they looked even more dangerous. I waved back with a no but he came towards me quickly followed by the small yapping dog. The dog looked old and tired and I could see it had a bit of a limp. The old man was carrying a well-used plastic bag. He had one of his hands in it and out of the bag he took half an apple and gave it to me. The apple had started to go brown, it looked like it had been cut a long time ago but I felt it too rude to refuse. He asked me in his very bad English "Are you, tourist?" I said yes and then I do not know why but answered him back in Turkish. Straight away, from my accent, the old man knew that I was a Cypriot. He then looked down at the dog and told her to say hello to me. He told me that the dog's name was Num Num after the sounds he heard of bullets being fired at each other whilst in combat. He told me that I could call her Ashkim because it meant lover and he loved her more than anything. He continued to tell me she had dementia and may not recognize her name. This Num Num was given to him by a rich family who were his customers when he lost Num Num number two. She was a runt of a litter of five and nobody picked her because of her disability but the family knew Isa loved his dogs so they gave her to him,

When I told him I had Cypriot parents he told me how he had lived in Kyrenia in Cyprus for six years after the war in 1974 and he knew Cyprus pretty well. I noticed that the old man had a foot missing. His legs looked well, very firm and muscled. The foot on his left leg was amputated. I tried to look away from this point, and carried on listening to him. He asked me how long I had been in Turkey, how long I was on holiday for and he then told me that I could find him in this spot every day and that the armchair was his, he had built it. He told me if I fancied grilled fish that I should not waste my money and come to him. He guaranteed its freshness and it was definitely the 'catch of the day'. I nodded, thanked him for the fruit and continued to walk back to my hotel. I held on to the apple until I was out of sight and threw it in the next litter bin that I found as I did not want to offend. Apple was not my favourite fruit anyway and I avoided healthy eating as much as I could.

I had seen the old man two other times before I found in myself the courage to walk down to him onto the rocks. These rocks were very uneven and slippery, many covered with green slimy seaweed. That day I also found out that the old man's name was Isa and that he was proudly homeless. He lived on the rocks and made a living off of what he could catch from below the waves with his two and a half-metre-long wooden rod. I noticed behind the rock sofa a single, child sized mattress and a boiling teapot.

Isa lived on the land but earned his living from the Bosporus. He would wake up every morning at 3:30am and set up then fished the Bosporus for two to three hours every day. He patiently fished through the harsh currents to catch enough fish that he knew that he could sell; he had regular customers who came to him daily. This was a busy fishing spot. All this would be done before sunrise. "It started as a hobby, but soon it became my living," said Isa as he pulled back his rod, lined all along with silver sardines. He smiled at me, "a rare catch in the Bosporus nowadays" he commented. He told me that he was a retired army officer and that the government did not do much to support the elderly, especially the disabled (looking down at his missing foot), so he was forced into changing his hobby into a way of living.

Isa was born in Istanbul. The Bosphorus was a big part of his life, ever since he could remember. Fishing and swimming was his life. They were the only things he said he was good at. When he mentioned swimming I told him how I had lost about five kilos in the past through swimming. He told me that the weight I was carrying was not good for me and that I should continue swimming. The more I looked and studied Isa, the more similarities I could see with my friend Ian in England. The old man sounded and even looked like my friend, they both had so much in common, and only their ages differed. Ian would have also nagged me, saying that I should "Carry on Swimming".

Ian was one of the part-time drivers who worked for New Opportunities at the day centre. About two weeks after starting I was asked by one of my team leaders that morning to do escorting with Ian. This was him driving around the community to various addresses picking up clients who were to attend the day centre that day. My job was to support the clients on and off the bus. I liked this part of the job, it was a time one could interact with a fellow staff member, talk about whatever thing was of interest that day and to me it was again one of those 'therapeutic moments' even though I hated the profession I was doing. Whilst on escorting duty, Ian and I would talk about 'everything and nothing' as they may say. Ian was such a great listener and we had so many things in common that I felt comfortable in his company. He was just someone to bounce off ideas and listen to me. Ian at the time was in a long term relationship, had spent the last few years bringing up his children as a lone parent and his eldest had just successfully completed university and he also loved football. We both had a lot in common, so I did not find it difficult to pass the monotonous and tedious time escorting which was quite demanding physically on me. I did not want anyone to know this, especially management, as they would soon have stopped allowing me to escort. On Fridays, after the 'run' we would both go to the local pub and sit down to chill out, carry on our gossiping and continue with more bravado. It was rather ironic that on an ordinary Friday afternoon, after work, I cannot remember how many times we got into conversation about our lives in the past and the future. But on this Friday, whilst talking about the same things such as our children and football, both of us who were from working-class backgrounds, not too studious when at school, discussed one day writing a book. The difference was Ian had almost finished his and I was still thinking about mine.

When I was about nine years old, my dad was a chauffeur for a rich Jewish businessman called Sam Sterling. Sam owned Sterling's Sportswear that made men's trousers. Because of my size, my dad thought I could find trousers that fitted me in the factory warehouse. Mr. Sterling seemed to like me and we started talking. I remember Mr. Sterling talking to me and was surprised that he treated me like an adult. When I told that him that I needed to go home to meet up with my mates he asked me in his very strong Jewish accent, "Mates?" and I nodded. He then out of nowhere, continued to tell me "Son when you, die, if you can name three good friends," showing me his hand with all fingers spread out, "you can call yourself; a lucky man!" Well, Ian was one that I could surely name. In the limited time I had known him he was and became a very good friend.

When I talked about my life with Ian, Ian brought it to my attention the fact that I blamed almost all the bad things in my life on my obesity and my mental state. Ian told me that he went swimming every Sunday and that I should go with him. The first question I asked him was if that time for swimming was an Adult only swim, or were there any children there? He said there would be no children. So I gave him my word that I would go with him. When I got to the changing room that first Sunday, I was shocked and got anxious. The public swim had just finished and children were still changing back into their clothes. I looked at Ian, but did not want to give away my cowardly feelings and took my clothes off, not caring who was looking at me. It was the first time in my life that I started a regime to better myself and carried it on for over a year. Apart from the exercise, swimming became very remedial. It was a time to escape and go into deep thoughts, focusing on just reaching different goals and blanking out life for that moment, forgetting what I was suffering. Swimming's purpose was to blank out all the internal pain.

Ian and I shared a love for watching football and this was a good reason to spend time with him. Our relationship was more than a friendship. He was a sort of unpaid semi-personal trainer

169

and mentor. His presence, without him saying anything verbally, kept me on track with my healthy living regime. He reminded me that I was on a diet and I would not dare to eat too much in front of him. He gave me the mental strength not to give up and to carry on. It was this period of my life when I had managed to realize one of my ambitions in my life, which was more luck than an achievement. I had been offered a season ticket by Arsenal football club, a very, very rare opportunity. Going to football and seeing Arsenal play at the Emirates stadium was 'the complete escape' and preparing to go to the match, walking to the stadium, was all great exercise. It got me out of the house and I was happy to be doing something objective, burning up calories. Most of the time as I walked to the ground I was in physical pain, my legs trembling, the left leg dragging the arthritis-ridden right one along. Then I would get a pain in my chest and the heavy breathing would start but the adrenalin of getting to see the game would always get me there. I could not have managed this if I had not started swimming.

The two hours or so whilst in the stadium were always beneficial. I would totally forget the mental state I was in, not remembering my problems, my love for H and the baggage that came with trying to be with her. My first game at the Emirates stadium, with my own season ticket, was without doubt one to remember. I got so excited I entered the turnstile, knowing that it would be a tight fit and turned my body sideways thinking it would fit me. It did not and I got stuck in between the turnstile, I could not even walk out backward, as the gates jammed. I was sandwiched between two seven feet high metal barriers. To add to the embarrassment an alarm started ringing to attract the attention of the stewards to help me. The sound of the bells also brought to the interest of other supporters that someone was in trouble. I only heard the laughter of others who thought it was funny that I was stuck. I was finally released, in minutes, but it felt like hours. I once again felt sick within myself. Throughout the match, I could not find myself enjoying this well-awaited moment, even though we were winning.

Going swimming towards the end had become tough work and monotonous. Finding the motivation to step out of the mood I was in became harder and harder. I needed a lot of prompting, mostly by Ian. I would, though, try and swim weekly and I used it as an excuse to have a shower afterward. I had lost the will to even wash. I would wash only if I could smell myself. Once I was in the water, swimming became a time of reflecting on what had passed, it became a time of mind games. Thinking, and more thinking, I found myself trying so hard not to hate. Mostly it was H that was on my mind, hating myself for being such a 'mug', hating myself for being so weak, hating me for being so wasteful. Hating me was easy. I did not want though, to fall into the trap of getting so low that I hated anyone. I did not want to hate H. Hiding this pain was like pretending and play-acting and is one of the hardest things to do.

Isa told me how he was a champion swimmer when he was in school and thought he would be world champion before he was conscripted into the army. He commented that it was unheard of for a World Champion swimmer to come from Turkey. Isa had a habit of going into conversation on one subject and changing to another, very quickly and I had, at times, trouble keeping up with the conversation, so just nodded politely. Isa would come to the Bosphorus to either fish or swim – he saw the Bosphorus as a way to get away from his bullying and dominant father, who verbally abused him. His father would always call him an idiot, or stupid, telling him he should make up a placard and hang it around his neck saying

"I'm stupid" and then go and walk around the fish market showing everyone what he was. Isa's mother did not escape her husband's behavior or intimidation but she would always tell Isa to respect his father and to get him out of the house, sent him fishing. Isa was relieved when he reached the age of twenty-one and was called up to join the Army. He did not do very well at school, so put all his energy into his swimming, believing in his dream. His relationship with his father seemed to have affected him.

Isa was born on the 20th July 1952 which made him sixty years old. I was surprised because he looked much older. The exposure to the sun had not helped his skin, his grey beard also put years on his looks. This date was significant, because exactly one year into his conscription, on his birthday in 1974, he was part of the 39th Infantry Division that landed in Cyprus. Although Isa could not wait to go into the army, he had not anticipated that a year into his service, he would be going into war. Before he knew anything he was driving an M47 tank into Kyrenia. This is where he lost his foot when he disturbed a mine, buried in a field.

Isa told me that whilst in the military hospital he fell in love with a young nurse named Suzan. She did not know this at the time. Suzan had barely qualified and had very limited nursing experience but found herself in the frontline, tending and caring for the injured in this new war. Suzan helped Isa slowly recuperate from his loss. Whilst in recovery, he had a lot of time to think of the past. He thought a lot about his father, in particular remorsefully regretting telling his father that he hated him and blamed him for destroying his life just before he had left to go to Cyprus. He could not come to terms with certain issues and at the time still blamed his father for rejecting him and making him so insecure, making him lose confidence. He remembered as a child the days his father promised to spend time with him, but only took him as far as the local Turkish Tea house where his father would spend hours drinking tea and playing cards with his friends. Isa would sit in the corner reading the same old newspapers and magazines people had left there again and again. Isa's main concern though, whilst lying in the hospital bed, was what was going to now happen after losing a foot?

Three weeks ago he was at the top of his prime; he was in the army, proud to be representing his country, wearing the uniform, fighting for the country he loved. He felt in control, he felt worthy and respected. The army trusted him and they gave him the responsibility of being in command of millions of pounds of military equipment. Now he was, once again, a 'nobody'. His Army days were over. Would he be able to swim again? How would he walk? He also knew that in Turkey disability was taboo, there was very little in social benefits, he would never be able to get married, have children or a job. He would now have to work for himself for survival.

BILLY G

Uncle must have been about seventy years old. He had wrinkle-free young skin, olive in colour. He could have been younger. He was slim. Billy G was over 6ft tall, with jet black hair and grey spread irregularly around his scalp, with a face sporting a crescent-shaped moustache and bushy eyebrows. You could say, a very Turkish looking man. Most of the time he looked very despondent and there seemed to be a heaviness about him. Most evenings you would find him sitting outside the doorway of his hotel, or inside in the foyer of the hotel behind the counter of the reception area. After eating my usual sea bass dinner, I would walk across and sit beside him and we would start talking. He asked the usual questions like, had I had a good day or had I seen the latest football results. He seemed to show an interest in the English Premier League and knew a lot about it. He told me he supported Newcastle United because they reminded him of his favorite Turkish team, Besiktas. He knew I supported Arsenal and he would remind me how badly we were playing that season.

After a few conversations, I found out that Billy G was a widower. His wife had died over forty years ago, whilst giving birth to his daughter. The little girl died thirty-six hours later from complications of being born prematurely. Billy G never remarried, his excuse was that 'it was written' and there was nothing he could do about it. He loved his wife and was saddened that he did not get the opportunity to get to know his child. Billy G also told me that he had a younger sister, Pinar, who lived somewhere around the world. She was about twenty years younger than him. They had not spoken for many months. His sister and he had disagreed on an issue and that it had not been resolved. Billy G said that he had a problem understanding her behaviour at times but put it down to the big gap in their ages. He loved her dearly because she was his only sibling and his blood. He felt his sister was a lot braver than him; she would take risks, try to better herself. At first he felt his sister was a confused woman but over the past twenty years had learned to understand her ways more. It was obvious that the matter of him falling out with his sister had been hurting him for a long time and been a burden to him.

Pinar was all the family he had left. Billy G said that he had raised her like his daughter, as he was much older than her. Whilst their mother and father were being occupied with the running of the hotel downstairs he would look after his little sister, washing her, dressing her, cooking her breakfast and generally looking after her. This way of life was the way until she went on to school. Things changed when Billy G got married and he tried to concentrate on his marriage which ended in the tragic way it did. Pinar quickly grew up, got herself an education and made her choices. Pinar married a very rich Tunisian man who was much older than her but had the financial resources to provide Pinar with all the needs and desires she craved. I never did find out why the two siblings were not talking at the moment. I suspected it was about the hotel. The only thing Billy G told me was that he got a phone call from his sister shouting through the phone and calling him a loser, who had 'sponged' off their parents all his life and that she would never talk to him again.

As I listened to Billy G's situation I realized that Billy G humbly accepted that he should have dealt with the situation better but did not expect that his sister would behave and disrespect him the way she did. He was obviously broken-hearted, he was her elder and it hurt! Over the long months that passed the pain did not get any easier. Since losing his wife and child, falling out with his only relative made Billy G a broken man. He just said that family quarrels have a total bitterness that cannot be matched by any other. But you must believe it is not for keeps and it can be resolved. The hotel business was what kept him alive.

The building had been owned by the family for as long as he could remember. It started off as the family home, renting out rooms to local fisherman, with any profits put into expanding the building into what it was now. Billy G did not remember when all the rooms were rented out to full capacity, but claimed with the cleaning and maintenance bills, he would be lucky to balance the books each year. He said developers had offered him fortunes to sell up, even offering proposals to him to rent the building out. He was adamant that would never happen.

I noticed that Billy G had the same T-shirt on since I first saw him, five days ago. I never saw him eat in any of the restaurants, or smoke. I felt that Billy G lived a very frugal life. The more I got to know him, the more I realized how unhappy Billy G was. He admitted to me that he was hurting and been in emotional pain for longer than he could remember. At times I was surprised how Billy G was opening up to me. He did explain in a somber way that whilst he could feel pain he knew that he was still alive. He admitted that he lived the way he did as a way of punishing himself and could not stop hurting himself, as he did not deserve a better life. He blamed himself for the death of his wife and felt a great loss in burying his child; he was ashamed that he and his only living relative had not got on together and would constantly have disagreements and not speak to each other for months or even years.

These conversations with Billy G would haunt me when I went to bed and I would often dream about what he said to me. It was as if Billy G was a mirror image of me. I understood how tormented Billy G was. The many nights I would find myself sitting outside the hostel I looked from a distance and thought about Billy G's life, comparing it to mine. It was ironic. Billy G would talk, or greet at least two hundred passersby throughout the evening but he admitted to me that he felt empty and alone, even though he was surrounded by people. He felt misunderstood by those around him and yearned for someone who could reach out to him and touch his heart. Billy G was in despair and very lonely. He believed and accepted that his life was over. He never ever wanted to get into another relationship again because at the end there would be an inevitable breakdown, either ending in divorce or death. He kept on saying that "Relationships would always end in heartbreak".

During my seventh night in Istanbul I had eaten my fish supper in my usual restaurant then crossed over the road to meet up with Billy G. He sent me back, asking me to order a bottle of good wine of my choice from the restaurant opposite and to bring it across to him with two glasses. Even the waiter in the restaurant was surprised. He commented "Uncle Ersen must like you," looking at me. "I have never seen that before" the waiter continued. Billy G told me it was his birthday and when I asked how old he was, he just ignored me, shrugging off the question by calling over to the waiter to bring over a bowl of mixed salty nuts and telling the waiter that he did not want to see the price of the nuts on his bill.

During this day there had been a bomb explosion in Taksim square, which was only a few miles from where we were, caused by a suicide bomber. The television in the foyer was on and all could hear the news broadcaster from outside, announcing that they had identified the bomber and where he was from. Billy G then started to comment by saying how quickly the bombing forensic teams were on the scene. They gathered evidence, put whatever they found in bags, such as clothing and blown up bits of flesh. The police quickly investigated it and they could identify who the bombers were. He then profoundly said, "Whatever you leave behind in life, will really tell a story about your life." After two small glasses of wine, Billy G started telling me that he felt empty and abandoned, nobody cared about him. I felt such a hypocrite telling him that things can always get better, even if they were bad now. Things are constantly changing. I told him that all though we did not always have control over things at the moment only he had the power over what direction his life takes. My point was that things can get better, there are no guarantees in life but there is the chance that it will. I felt so bad within myself. I felt like such a fraud. I could not even believe that I was saying these things to him.

Billy G was the first person I asked about the subject of a gun, maybe it was because I thought it unlikely he would help me get one. I had noticed a lot of regular Turkish-speaking men loiter around the local streets and standing on the corners doing nothing but harass the tourists, mostly females, offering themselves as personal tour guides. One of these young men was very distinguished and loud. I asked Billy G about him. Was this certain man a member of the Turkish Mafia? This particular gentleman was regularly hanging around the area, confident; he was very flashy and wore a smart suit. He would often be drinking Raki, on his own, looking around the area inquisitively, chain-smoking and playing with his black and white worry beads. I never ever noticed him paying for any of his drinks. Billy G just grinned and told me "That's the local idiot. Sometimes he mingles with tourists and encourages them to spend money at the bars so he'd get tips from the restaurant owners. 90% of the time he is drinking water, waiting for unsuspecting punters. The suit he was wearing was the same one he had found when a guest had forgotten a suitcase and never returned to collect it." I then asked Billy G how much the Mafia would charge to kill somebody in Istanbul. Billy G told me that someone like me or him they would kill for 100ytl (£40). I laughed at that. I then thought I would ask where I could get a gun. Billy G solemnly just asked me who I was going to kill. I again just laughed at the question, trying to distract from the fact that I was serious. I left the matter there. I felt that Billy G liked me and showed me respect, so I did not want to look stupid or unstable by giving him a clue as to what my intentions were.

My relationship with Billy G grew by the day and he became a sort of substitute mother and father figure. He was the first person I would speak to in the mornings, always in the foyer. Sometimes I used to think that he used to sleep in the foyer, my eyes often wandered around the foyer looking for a sign of a bed. When I left my room in the mornings, he would greet me by saying "Good morning son," asking me what my plans were for that day. In the evenings, Billy G would be the last person I spoke to. He would wish me a good night and always end the day by telling me to "Leave it to God". Leave what to God? Those four last words were very moving in that I would question what was Billy G actually saying? At first I thought, was this just a habit, like one says Good Night, as in him being polite and well mannered? Was he telling me that I should go to bed and go to sleep and whilst asleep leave the running of the world and it's affairs to God? Or was he telling me to go to bed, switch off, and leave all my problems and feelings to God and that God would solve them? Leave it to

God? Would God heal the hurting pain, would He take away the animosity and burden of the past fifty years of living and carrying around the weight of three normal men? Will God unravel the hate, anger, and bitterness that I had towards myself and mankind? Did Billy G know how I was feeling and did he know of the struggles that were bothering me? Or was he just engulfed in his own issues and could not find a solution for his own personal problems and was now resorting to leaving it to divine powers, to find answers.

It was interesting in that Billy G was at times a strong man, mentally and other times showed weaknesses in his character. At times he would give out an aura of being in control, especially around his immediate environments, powerfully willed. Another time Billy G would become honestly humble and be so transparent and show his insecurities. I would always reflect about Billy G and what we had spoken about, maybe it was because he was the last person I had contact with before retiring for the night. As I lay on my bed, I wondered and asked why Billy G was the way he was, comparing him with Vedat and Isa. Billy G had the capability of buying anything that he wanted although I was not sure he knew it or accepted it. He was a very charismatic man and he could attract any woman. I tried to evaluate Billy G's life circumstances with mine.

This was a time to think, plan my strategies as I lay on the bed, looking at that ceiling, again. I knew all the cracks, damp patches, and now had become friends with the moth circling the light bulb. I started talking to it, I never knew if it was the same moth but I named it Jane. Jane was the last counselor that I had sought help from. She was also part of work's occupational health service. I had referred myself because I felt I was in the last stages of self-destruction, was desperate for help. I knew that I had reached rock bottom. Jane had telephoned me to discuss the possibility of us both spending some time together and invited me to her surgery. She told me that she worked from home and asked me if I was okay with that. She gave me the address, stipulating that she practiced at 12A and that I should not go to door number 12. Also that she would most probably have had a client before me, so I should be on time, not early or late. Well, I did go first to door 12, knocking and getting no reply. When I eventually found the right door, 12A, I rang the bell, five minutes late. When Jane opened the door, and I proudly, with a smile, confessed my mistake to Jane, apologizing for my lateness, she was not impressed. This was my third set of therapy sessions with a different counselor throughout my life. I had become familiar in counseling styles and knew what to expect on our first session with Jane but surprisingly she was the first one who confirmed to me that I had a mental health issue.

She quickly diagnosed me with Oppositional Defiance Disorder. She explained her opinion to me and my so-called prognosis. I thought she was making it up as she was talking about it. The more I thought about her theory, the more I believed her. She said that it was like a person who was just rebellious and anti-establishment. Children may suffer from ODD but soon grow out of it. I obviously did not. I liked what she was saying because at last I had an answer that explained the simple reasons as to why I behaved the way I do. I found it very useful now I was being informed by a therapist that I was suffering from a disorder called "Opposition Defiance Disorder (ODD). I quickly rushed away after the session to investigate, and to see if this really existed. Having read up information about the prognosis, I started thinking and analyzing myself for the first time. It all made sense to me. I was supposed to have five cognitive behavioral therapy sessions. I ended up having ten. The next nine sessions Jane would just sit opposite me, virtually motionless, listening to me for almost an hour, looking at me and not saying much, just nodding. I often left the surgery feeling worse than when I went in. We both agreed at the end that we had failed to explore the deep personal problems which I had in the time allowed. She recommended that I should carry on looking into having further counseling. Whilst lying on that bed in that room, I would talk to the moth telepathically, but like Jane, the moth would just be looked down at me, saying nothing.

I was as confused as ever at what life was about. Here I was, running away from my problems, as I could not find any answers. I started to think more about why I had decided to end it. H had ripped me apart emotionally and my ego and self-esteem were at its lowest ever. Losing H was demoralizing, I felt worthless, I felt so ugly. I thought to myself, no one would ever fancy a fat man, let alone fall in love with one. I had got so used to rejection and defeat. I had lost any strength to take any more risks or the courage to gamble. I was that emotionally messed up that the idea of suicide felt good. I thought however, ludicrous, that killing myself would make all those who said they loved me at the time and had rejected me, feel guilty and suffer some of the pain I was experiencing

The guilt of leaving my children's mother for another woman had started to bother and haunt me more and more now that the relationship with H had finished. For the past twenty years, I had never consciously recognized that I had hurt a blameless woman who had given me two children. I then punished my daughters, for no reason but for my lust. When H was with me, even when I was just hanging onto what we had together, everything else was insignificant and everyone around me was irrelevant.

182

Family and friends that knew or suspected that I was still in some sort of relationship with H never before expressed any opinion on my so-called friendship with her. I can somewhat imagine why they thought not to, but as soon as it became common knowledge that the relationship was over, their comments and opinions made me realize how much my obsession with H had made me so disenfranchised with anything else. I was lost and felt so ashamed. I found myself questioning my intelligence and talking to myself, calling myself stupid. Most of all I could now see how much I had let my children down, in those lost years of making H my obsession, making her my living idol, my God. My addictive compulsion for her seriously blurred my thinking, even when gambling I would lose control, not thinking of consequences.

On one of our many getaway weekends, it was one of those exceptional occasions that H and I were out and about, not hiding in the flat or a hotel room. We were both passing time in an amusement arcade and H was trying to topple a pile of two pence pieces from one of the amusement games. For me that was a waste of time, I was in the Adults 18 Only section playing for a big return. I struck lucky and had won the jackpot on a fruit machine which was £500 but instead of walking away and enjoying this very, very rare moment, I went onto a further gambling establishment and in a few minutes lost all the winnings. I was so engrossed in my own world, my bubble, blinded to reality.

Since coming to Istanbul, I had started to see how much I had ignored my responsibilities of being a father. How could I repay my daughters back? I knew when I killed myself my employers would have to payout a death in duty award, which would benefit my children. Would this have been any consolation for the abuse I had inflicted on them? Because of the way things turned out, I felt I owed Honey more than Gemma, Gemma lived with me, until she went on to university, whilst Honey stayed with her mother. I definitely did not give Honey as much as I gave Gemma, materially as well as spiritually. Gemma may not agree with me but I am sure Honey missed out on what I gave her sister. Both my daughters had been successful in what they were doing and both had now developed immensely different personalities, better than I deserved. However I still felt guilty for divorcing their mother and behaving the way I had. Throughout the past two decades I believed that I had been a good father, H would always tell me that I was a great provider, a great father but an awful husband. When reflecting, I knew I was not a good father neither was I a good husband. Being an absent father throughout most of my children's lives - more so Honey's life - was another label I had to contend with.

Vedat told me that when I spoke about this, however much I tried to undermine or even joke about my feelings, he could see the anger in me, the emptiness, the sadness, and the heaviness. He told me that I was obviously heartbroken, because of the ending of a romantic relationship. I was feeling the loss of something real, something that I had hoped for. He told me that hearts will always get broken, he told me that heartbreak was like an iceberg, one fifth was on the outside but the rest was in the inside and how you feel emotionally can determine how one feels physically. Vedat unremittingly instructed me that if I wanted to feel better, I needed to take three steps to get the best out of life: firstly, I should accept and face my past without any regret. Secondly, I should start dealing with and handling the present with some confidence and thirdly, that I should start to prepare myself for the future without any fear.

Billy G and Vedat were very good teachers and had immense mentoring skills. They both had grand skills in teaching on whatever they knew. They both possessed great life knowledge and both had made some sort of achievement in their life. Billy G had maintained the family business and his property was worth a lot more than when he had inherited it. Whereas Vedat from childhood had learned and survived life on his own, he had a great wife, children, and grandchildren. He worked very hard in running and maintaining a small business and had educated his children. But to me Isa was different. He glowed with compassion, empathy and patience. He felt that he had not achieved anything in his life. But I saw that his life was full of achievements. The fact that he never lost his enthusiasm for life was very inspirational. I found myself sitting by him for hours and hours just listening to what he had to say.

Whenever we were together, we swapped past experiences I told him of my past, he would listen patiently and later talk to me about his. He continued to tell me that as he was convalescing in hospital, his love grew daily for Suzan. He did not think she knew of his feelings, but he knew. He was in love for the first time. He started to get worried and anxious when there was talk that he could be moved soon as by that time a ceasefire had been declared and that he would be flown back to Turkey. He knew it would be for further physiotherapy, but what thereafter? On the 'scrapheap' as he put it. He needed to stay in Cyprus. Formalities and rules meant that all war casualties had to return back to a Turkey homecoming, back to a hero's welcome. Well, the hero's welcome lasted ten minutes. He defiantly was not a hero with his father. His father showed him no compassion and told him that he had returned back to Istanbul as a cripple, blaming him for what had happened to him.

Isa promised himself that he would revisit to Cyprus as soon as he could. He was awarded a war pension and as soon as it came through and had built up to a healthy amount, he flew immediately back to Cyprus and headed back to the hospital. It was as if he had not left, almost everyone he had left behind was still there. Most importantly, Suzan! She was still nursing the injured. Casually he got the courage and asked her if she wanted to go for a drink or something to eat after she finished her shift. She said yes and it was the best moment of his life. He knew he wanted to stay in Kyrenia for the rest of his life. He thought to himself, ironically he wanted to spend the rest of his life where he had experienced the worst tragedy of his life.

He found a job in a fish restaurant, based in a big hotel. He would fish for the restaurant at the break of dawn and be a waiter in the evenings. He lived free in a room provided by the hotel. The arrangement suited him as he could visit the hospital during the day. He eventually got the courage to tell Suzan how he felt about her and stated his intentions. He knew and felt straight away that Suzan did not have the same feelings for him and hated himself for allowing him to be rejected in life once again. Suzan loved him, but was not in love with him, seeing him as a patient that she respected. He thought to himself he would save some money and return back to Istanbul. He ended up staying in Cyprus for six years, only returning when he heard that his mother had died and he needed to return back for her funeral.

Isa's arrival back to Istanbul was not a good one. Not only did he have to bury his mother, he had no choice but to go back home to be confronted with his father. His first feeling of dejection was when he tried to unlock the front door with what he thought was his house key, that he carried with him wherever he went. Until that moment of time he believed that was his home. The locks had been changed and he knew from that point on it was time for him to move on. What Isa did not say verbally was expressed to me through his eyes and facial expressions. Finding the door locks changed had obviously hurt him and that was the last day he stayed at his home. In a few minutes his family home had become his father's home. Before leaving the family home Isa attempted to kiss his father's hand as a gesture of respect, after all, he was his father, but his father refused to give him his hand. Isa said that when he walked out of his father's house, he looked up at the sky, raised both arms and thanked God it was summer, he was ready to live rough and the weather would help. He never ever returned back home. As long as Isa was concerned, 'it was finished'. Isa never planned to live on the rocks, of the Bosphorus but said the rocks were calling for him.

Not long afterwards he found a spot that he liked, and proudly smiled at me, calling where he was standing his Nirvana. It was where he had now found his dominion. He asked me what my Nirvana was. I laughed and he asked me what my definition of paradise was. At that moment of time, I had no answer. I just shrugged my shoulders. He then said something that made me think; "Some people are in paradise and do not know it". Mind you, a lot of what Isa told me whilst we were together often made me reflect. Isa soon became friends with the stray cats and kittens who were born and lived on the rocks. His best friend though was Num Num. This Num Num was his third baby since moving onto the rocks. The winters were the hardest, it could get as cold as -15deg C at night and he told me how they both would cuddle up together in a gap between the rocks, keeping each other warm. Num Num had been his life-saver more than once.

Isa's story was so inspiring, I used to forget how scared I was of the rocks and how difficult I found climbing them. Even sitting on them was uncomfortable. Now I would sit on them for over eight hours and time would just fly past. Isa told me that living on the rocks had given him freedom that could not be explained, he felt so safe. He described his life as walking on a long thin tightrope, thousands of feet in the air, knowing that if he would fall, there was a safety net below. He was sure not to be hurt. He never worried about anything, he believed and had complete and utter faith that all his needs would be provided. He had been saved from any more torment, ever again. At first he saw that each day was a new day, he felt life had become surreal in that oddly, he would wake up in the morning, opening his eyes and waiting for that day to be a bad day, so he could curl up into depression, feeling sorry for himself and mentally start hurting again. It took him ages to get used to the freedom and the control that he had in his life. He then told me a story. I loved all these stories.

"Rimante and Domas were a beautiful couple in love. Both lived for each other. They lived on the ground floor of a three-story house. Above them lived the couple's widowed landlord. Rimante was a housewife and Domas was working as a waiter in a restaurant. Every day after work Domas would go to the local delicatessen and with the tips he accrued that day, buy a bottle of wine. If he had a good day financially he would buy two. He would also buy food and meze for that night. Rimante and Domes would sit in the garden in the evenings, eating and drinking. They would soon start getting merry and Domas would take out his guitar and start playing. Rimante would start singing and dancing. Upstairs the landlord would sit at his window and watch the happy couple. This would upset and infuriate the landlord.

The landlord was visiting an old friend and whilst chatting told his friend of his dilemma. He told him that he had all the money he needed. He owned property, did not need anything but was still very unhappy. Whereas his tenants who lived downstairs owned nothing, had very little money but were happier and had a better life than him. The landlord explained to his friend about the singing and dancing every night. The friend then suggested that the landlord should get a big glass jar and half-fill it with silver coins. He told the landlord to give the jar to the couple and tell them if they can fill the rest of the jar with silver coins, they could keep the jar. The landlord liked the idea.

So this is what the landlord did. He knocked on the couple's door knowing that Rimante was home but her husband was at work. The landlord had the half-filled jar with him. He told Rimante about his idea and that the jar was a gift that they could keep with the condition that the couple filled the other half of it with silver coins. Rimante looked at the jar and it made her very happy and excited. When Domas came home that night from work with the wine and food, Rimante told him about the jar. She told him that from now on they were going to save all his tips. Change them into silver coins and fill up the jar. Domas agreed and this is what they did.

The next day there was no wine, no meze, no music, no more singing and dancing. The landlord would look from his window above and smile at how he had taken control of the situation".

Isa told me this is how cruel society can be if you allowed it. Often I would find myself drifting off into my own thoughts and thinking about how my life was and why I had come to Istanbul. Well, I knew why. But what was the final straw? How had the last days in London impacted? Here was Isa, he had made a conscious decision to stay out of the 'rat race' of civilisation, had chosen what kind of life he wanted to live in it and seemed to me that he had found what I had been looking for all my life, which was gratification. Isa had found the truth of life and this fact had set him free. I was so envious of him, I wanted this understanding also. Finding the knowledge of life would have given me liberation.

With Billy G, I could not help but to be withdrawn. I knew of his sorrow and just listened, I was surprised that he was so open with me, and I felt it hard to tell him about my failings and inadequacies. My relationship with Vedat, on the other hand, was more balanced and relaxed. I liked the way he quickly showed faith in me. Vedat was in a stage in his life that I could envy. Maybe if I would have made it to his age, would have looked at the past and said to myself "That was good!" Vedat was always shining, he was pure. I knew that I had to listen to what Vedat was saying and trusted it. However because of this purity I held back in what I could tell him about myself. Maybe it was because I was ashamed, or in some sort of denial or that I knew he would have not agreed with my opinions or approved of my past actions.

With Isa, the association was simply an education. The more I saw Isa, the more I could not help myself but focus and be drawn in by his eyes. Isa had bigger eyes than usual, brown eyes, with the whites in his eyes perfectly clear and forever twinkling. At first, I thought these faultless eyes were the result of him swimming consistently in the salt water of the Bosporus, but I later started to see his eyes for what they really were. These eyes were made of love. Isa's aura of love overflowed. Isa helped me regain my self-reliance, to start becoming honest, especially with myself and I started to open up emotionally, finding myself speaking freely about everything without any restrictions. Isa was very perceptive and got angry with me whenever I went into my 'clown' mode. He asked me why I kept on doing it, why did I become a child, did I not realise I was over fifty years old? He told me there was nothing wrong with laughing or having a sense of humor, but when I became this joker, to him it was obvious I was using this emotion to distract the listener that I was not happy with the situation I found myself in, or that I was becoming withdrawn. It took me time to analyze what he was saying but I understood it later on and I tried to stop being the comedian of the party. I found myself having a more mature attitude around him.

Isa was not always the mentor, giving me his experienced opinion, or trusted advice. He also had the gift of compassion. I often found myself crying in front of him and many times Isa would also cry with me. It was very comforting to see a tear running down Isa's cheek, which showed me that as well as listening, he had empathy with how I felt at the time. Isa brought to my attention that I had, over the years, adopted many unhelpful thinking habits. When he described his observations about me, I could not help but laugh at what he was saying because I agreed with him. Isa said that sometimes I was a bit of a clairvoyant, a mind reader.

At times I assumed that I knew what others thought about me, which was usually negative. I had also created a 'mental filter' which meant that I only noticed what I wanted to, or what my mind had allowed me to become aware of and that I would dismiss anything that did not fit. I was looking out into the world, with blinkers, or 'depressing specs' only catching the negative stuff, like a tea strainer and ignoring the good, positive or realistic bits and pieces flowing into the glass. I made evaluations or judgments about myself, others or actions rather than describing what I actually saw and could verify. I had lost touch with any emotional reasoning. I feel bad, so it must be bad. I had adopted a habit of putting myself down, self-criticizing; blaming myself for what had passed or happened that were not my responsibility.

The current situation and events were triggering upsetting memories. Isa told me that I should stop seeing the world as black and white, believing that something or someone can only be good or bad, right or wrong, rather than anything in-between or shades of grey. Whilst he was talking to me, I started to take my shoes and socks off. Isa looked at me and asked what I was doing. I told him that I wanted to dangle my feet in the sea, because the blisters on my feet were becoming sore and that the salty sea water would help them heal quicker. Isa then asked me why I did not go into the sea and have a swim. I immediately shook my head saying no. Isa reminded me that I said I could swim, what was I afraid of? I went quiet. I looked out into the sea. Isa then asked, me when was I going to stop this hiding? I looked at him in silence. Isa asked me why I ran away from trying new things, like swimming in the Bosporus as it was obvious to him I wanted to do it. I looked around to see who was around and thought, should I? I felt ashamed and scared but felt that I wanted to prove Isa wrong that I was not hiding. I knew I was reluctant to take my top off and go into the water. Isa just looked at me with his wide penetrating eyes, waiting. The more he looked, the more I wanted to prove him wrong. Isa then continued to lecture me about hiding from myself; society did not care about my size, why did I worry what other people think? Those hours that I spent sitting on the rocks, looking out to the sea, watching the boats go past, ships gliding along the waters; I must have watched thousands of people each day, none of them aware of me studying and trying to analyze them. Isa continued to tell me, "When one rebels out of society, disobeying the human race – you start living in what you create". Isa was living on the rocks, content and humbly happy. In my case, it led to emptiness, ugliness, resentment. I had started to recognize a pattern developing here in Istanbul and at the time could not understand why.

I then decided to take my top off and walked to the edge of the water. Before I knew it I was walking on the rocks, getting deeper and deeper into the water, until I had no choice but to swim. I had now found my Nirvana! I never felt so free! Hesitantly and slowly I swam away from the shore, for a split second thinking that I would swim further out, as far as I could and not make it back. I looked towards Isa and saw he just carried on doing his own thing, not looking towards me. The water became comforting the longer I was in it. It was a perfect temperature and I had escaped from everything for a moment. I stayed in the water until my skin on my fingers started to prune, I did not want to get out. The current was pushing me towards the shore and then I was brought back to the real world. I swam back to the shore as close as I could and tried to stand and walk out of the sea. The rocks under my feet started to slip, I could not walk out, I was stuck. I tried to swim in closer, I could feel my belly touching the rocks beneath me. I tried to stand up but my arms could not carry my weight and the rocks beneath me were too loose. I could not get out. I looked towards Isa but he was not aware that I was struggling. I looked around me for other people, not for help but I was worried and embarrassed that they would be looking at me, like I was a whale who was stranded. I had thoughts of the Turkish navy coming down to rescue me, or a crane being employed to get me out. Isa was by then too far from me to notice me and my predicament. I just crawled my way out, being helped by the waves of the sea pushing me closer onto the land. I eventually found the strength to get out of the water. As I sat on the hot rocks, breathing heavily, topless, sea water dripping of my torso looking at the sea, I had mixed feelings. I was happy and proud, I had made it! I swam in the Bosporus.

Then realism crept back in. I was too fat, I felt so useless. I kept these feelings to myself. I asked myself why I didn't carry on swimming into the paths of ferries. I was immediately reminded why I was in Istanbul. I used the salty water as an excuse to leave Isa, telling him I needed to go back and wash. Isa just nodded and said "Okay, you know what to do" and I walked away silently, not really listening.

The Bosphorus Disciples

It was a normal Friday evening in Istanbul. As usual, the roads and the Bosphorus ferry lanes were very busy, doing all the usual transporting of people back and forth. As I walked back the shorts that I was wearing were getting dryer. I thought about the last hour and what had happened. I needed to talk to Billy G about the room. Did I want it for a few days more, a week or maybe two? I was now more determined to do what I came to do. The question left, was when? When was I going to do it? There were things that had to be done. I felt that I had got to know Billy G well enough and he would not have minded if I stayed in his hotel longer. It was more about respect rather than a money issue. I did not want Billy G to think of me as someone taking advantage of his hospitality, besides which, I was also now running out of money. I thought it would have been over by now, so I had not budgeted in staying so long. I was still being paid by my employers, but next payday was not due for weeks. I needed to work out my timings.

I did not want to owe Billy G any money when my mind was made up. Thankfully it was the off peak period and there were many vacant rooms in the hostel. The next question was how I was going to do it now that I had made my mind up. Killing myself in Billy G's hotel room was not an option. Billy G did not deserve the burden of cleaning up after me if I chose to blow my brains out. I was no nearer to getting my hands on a gun anyway. Jumping of the bridge was out of the question. I was not physically fit enough to be able to access myself conveniently to jumping off any of the bridges. Standing in front of a tram was an easier option. This idea ticked all the boxes. It was accessible, it would have been quick, hopefully instant. I thought about carrying a letter on myself with all my personal details and my funeral wishes. A letter addressed to my daughters explaining why. The tram idea sounded good but then I thought about the feelings of the tram driver. He could lose his job, or be traumatized for killing someone. He may be a family man, he did not know who, or why I had come to this position. No! This was not a good idea. I was selfish, but this was my crisis, not the driver, who was trying to do a day's work. I did not want to create problems for this person who was doing a job to support his family. So, using the tram as a tool for committing suicide was also ruled out.

Before I went back to the hotel I looked out for Vedat to say my usual good night. By now saying goodnight had become a long ritual and Vedat would use this opportunity to leave the business to me, saying he needed to go to the toilet or speak to someone. Sometimes he would disappear for hours. I became a real expert in roasting chestnuts. As soon as I greeted Vedat he looked at me as he had never before and the first thing he asked me was if I was ok. I asked him why, did I look ill? He said no and told me that he saw me approaching him from a distance and I looked as if I was carrying the weight of the world on my shoulders. He then looked into my eyes and told me that he was waiting for me to come and run the stall, but he has changed his mind because he did not want me to scare the customers away. I laughed at what he said, but I did not want to talk about me anymore. I was thinking about things that I knew he would not have tolerated. He then started to talk to me like a father talking to his child, "Naci, do not kid me." I just looked at him. That was the first time since I had arrived in Istanbul that anyone had called me by my first name.

I was shocked. I did not even remember telling any person my name. Vedat always called me 'Tombull' (Chubby) before. I could not be offended by it as he was bigger than me. Billy G identified me as Sir, and although I was his junior, he never lost the 'I was the paying customer ethic'. Isa always called me my son or my child so it was very interesting being called by my name. Vedat continued to tell me, "You are not shining today, are you thinking of how to leave us?" I stepped back and asked "us?" wondering to myself and looking inquisitively. "Yes, leaving Istanbul?" Vedat continued. I told him that I had to go one day and Vedat just nodded. When I asked him why I would think on how I was leaving, he then told me he thought I may take the train back through Europe. I was now more confused. His voice then got louder and asked he asked me heatedly, "Have you learned nothing? Do you not understand the restlessness of your own spirit?" He continued to talk to me as if he was preaching. "You of all people know what it's like, your mind is always racing, always asking yourself, what are people thinking, what are they saying about you. You have tried this, you tried that- you tried everything. You know what is strange? You have been to many places looking for peace but on the inside you did not fit but on the outside you look like you are 'in' but deep down, you have something saying to you, you are not made for this. You think you're invisible. For decades you have spent your time feeding yourself to become bigger, so people can see you and notice you, so stop hiding if you want to be seen!"

I then really started to get scared. That word 'hiding' had come up again. He finished by asking me when I was going to wake up. He then told me that I could restore my lost years if only I wanted to. "You think your divorce killed, you. In fact, it actually saved you!" I found myself speechless and shocked, no words could come out of the mouth. I felt my lips trembling, my brain went into overload, all I knew was I had to go. I needed to get away from Vedat. This was the shortest time I had ever stayed with him. I said goodnight and walked off. Vedat just nodded, looking away from me, pretending that he was wiping his workbench and shaking his damp cloth. As I walked away I felt my throat drying up and I felt my eyes watering and tears running down my cheeks. I was now this fifty year old man and I was crying like a baby. Was I that transparent?

I arrived back at the hotel and as usual, Billy G was sitting in the doorway, worry beads in hand, watching over the passers-by. He looked at me as I was approaching and as usual, my attention was being called by competing waiters trying to entice me into their eating establishments. I could hear Billy G shouting out to them, "Can't you leave the man alone, pick on a tourist, and he is one of us! He has enough going on, he does not need your stupidity!" I just laughed as I got nearer to Billy G, greeted him and he was shaking his head as if he was fed up with the people around him. I asked him if he was staying there for the next few hours and he replied sarcastically, "No, I'm dining and wining that Ukrainian lass I met last night!" quickly followed by asking himself under his breath, "Do I go anywhere?" I told him that I was going to my room to freshen up and needed to talk to him later on. He nodded, asking me to bring him some English painkillers down from my room when I came back down, as he felt he had a headache coming on and he did not trust the ones that he had. "They were made in some sweatshop in Moscow," he said again in his sarcastic voice.

I went to my room, sat on the unmade bed and just put my hands in my face.. I closed my eyes as my body started to get hot and hotter and I began to sweat as I had never sweated before. I thought I was ill, my skin started to boil as if I had been sitting in the hot sun all day. Had I had an allergic reaction to the water in the Bosporus? I rushed into the shower room, stripping off as I got there, locked the door. Switched on the tap and put my head under the running tap. As the cold water gushed out over my head I tried to recall when in the last two weeks whilst in Istanbul, had I last been depressed? I could not remember. When did I have my last panic attack?

I no longer need H's love anymore, I was not hurting any longer and I do not hate myself! Fifty years on, I felt alive! But, what was happening here? It was not a feeling I had been used to. I kept on hearing Vedat's voice in my head and his last speech to me about me being 'invisible' and eating food to get bigger and bigger so people noticed me. What was that about? I detested my size, I hated what I was. I had become despondent with the world, rebelled because I felt that I had never, ever been recognized for me, always alone in my head, never acknowledged for what and who I was. Now I was hiding in a cheap hostel in Istanbul, thinking how to end it all. I just stood under the running shower with the temperature of the running water getting hotter and hotter. It did not matter, I could withstand, it I felt that I could take anything now, whatever the world wanted to throw at me. I was now being cleansed. I stood for what seemed to be hours under this misty silver coloured lime-scaled shower head, allowing the water to splash all over me. I had never ever submersed myself like this before. Even when I used to go swimming, I hated water splashing in my face.

When I came down to meet up with Billy G, he was still sitting where I left him. His first remark was I that he was going to call the council to declare a water shortage in the area. I looked at him, puzzled as he continued to say that if everyone stays in the shower room as long as me, Istanbul would run out of water. I asked him how he knew I was in the shower. He pointed at the down pipe above his head, which led to a drain, near him. I then asked how he knew it was me. He said I was the only one living there at the moment. We both laughed at the same time, then he told me that there was nothing like the deep cleansing of a soul. I thought to myself, whilst looking up at the stars in the sky, that I felt too drained and exhausted to comment or ask what he had meant by what he just said.

As I sat beside Billy G, thinking about the past events of that evening with Vedat and the shower I heard a mobile phone ringing. The ringtone was like a toy. Strangely then Billy G took out an old style mobile phone that was at least fifteen years old. I had never seen him with the phone before. What happened next was the scariest thing I had witnessed in my entire life; it was like the special effects of a science fiction film.

As soon as Billy G answered the phone and said hello to the caller, his misdemeanor visibly changed. I looked at him and for a split second my heart missed a beat and I got worried. All of a sudden his face brightened up and it started to glow, then I witnessed and heard the bones in his fingers that were holding the phone crack and the fingers started to straighten. He lifted his other hand and we both looked at it, together, the bones in that hand were cracking at the same time and his hands became perfect. Billy G looked at me, I looked at him. He then pressed the button on his phone whilst looking at his hands and he told me that the caller was his little sister and she had told him that she had been thinking of him and she loved him. I just looked at Billy G, stunned and speechless and thought I was dreaming. He just looked at his hands, they were both just right. Perfect. I just found myself wanting to walk away from him. He looked as if he had been cursed and all the curses had been lifted. I tried but could not speak and I just fell back into my chair. Billy G then stood up and started to walk, his limp had also gone. He then walked into the hotel and I did not have any strength to follow him. I was paralyzed and numb. I sat in the chair, waiting for him to return.

I woke up the next morning still sitting in the chair. I must have fallen asleep. At first I thought I had dreamt all that I had witnessed. I stood up, everything was as normal, the cafes were opening and the road sweeper was cleaning the streets. The odd thing was Billy G was nowhere in sight and it sort of confirmed that what I had experienced the night before was not a dream. Where was he? I got up and asked the nearest people if they had seen Billy G that morning. No-one said they had seen him. I walked into the hotel but there was nothing different from the night before. I looked at the clock in the foyer, it was still six thirty in the morning. I then went up to my room and it was as I left it. I thought it was still early so I would try and get some sleep and give Billy G time to wake up. I woke up after about three hours and expected Billy G to be awake and sitting downstairs in one of his usual places, but he was nowhere. I started to get curious and worried. I started thinking to myself, asking myself all sorts of questions, more importantly, where was Billy G?

I thought to myself, I will go and find Isa and spend some time with him. When I was with him although he was present, I could still think on my own, he would never question, or pressure me. I could sit on the rocks and think about what was happening and what I was going to do next. Usually, I would go and see Vedat first thing in the morning, simits tasted good when fresh, they had a doughy texture and you could taste and smell the sesame seed oils, with that slight hint of cinnamon. They would also be still hot or at least warm. That morning I was not sure if I wanted to see him and I was feeling guilty. The truth really does hurt in this situation. Avoiding Vedat would have been the coward's way out, I could catch up with him later on anyway. I did not know why but I felt I was a fraud and thought I may have upset him. Vedat had quickly become a friend, a father figure so trying to avoid him made me feel like I was betraying our friendship. Or was I now close to ending it and ashamed of my decision? Did Vedat know anything about what I was thinking?

I took the longer way round to go and meet up with Isa and strangely whilst walking I felt as if Vedat's eyes were watching me and that he could see that I was trying to avoid him. I felt his presence around me, I could even smell simits. Although I had taken a diversion, my eyes were in the area where he was pitched. He moved his stall around according to the weather, and if the business was slow, he would go and tempt the fishermen to buy him out. Some mornings, he would go around giving away yesterday's unsold simits to the fisherman to use as bait. So he could have been anywhere. This morning though, Vedat was nowhere to be found. This made the morning easier for me but scary at the same time, no Billy G or Vedat.

I met up with Isa. He had not disappeared and as usual he was topless, moisturizing his torso with his own concocted moisturizer made with a mixture of olive oils and pureed fruit. I could see that he had caught that day's business and wrapped it up; it was hidden in the shade. When I saw Isa I greeted him and told him what I had experienced the night before outside the Hotel and asked him what he thought. Isa told me that bitterness and pain will always trouble family relations. Isa continued to ask me if I had ever tried to maintain a growing relationship with a person who was rooted in bitterness. He continued to explain to me how easy this could be done because that person is absorbed with these detrimental feelings about someone else. More to the point, it is hard to spend time with anyone who is consumed by bitterness, for the reason that such people simply, cease being likable.

Bitterness comes from being angry and from hatred. Bitterness gets worse when one refuses to let go when someone or something is taken from them. I remember Isa saying something that was so profound that it put me into a trance. He said "Bitterness is being constantly hurt by memory and holding onto it until it has a hold on you" and he continued to explain to me how bitterness is one of the unhealthiest emotions one can have. When you are offended or disappointed by others and you allow that hurt to germinate in your heart, bitterness and resentment will take root. Bitterness is characterized by an unforgiving spirit and generally negative, critical attitudes. What happens to them physically? Can one get physically sick? Isa continued to explain to me and it was as if he knew Billy G. The bitterness may have caused arthritis to develop in Billy G's bones. Suppose it is bitterness towards a member of his family that he kept within, nurturing it, not sharing it. He had kept it all buried inside him. Now it was suppressed inside him for so many years, the hurt finally begins to physically show itself visibly.

At that time my thoughts immediately returned to me and my past. There was a lot of bitterness around my life that I now recognized. I was unforgiving and bitter at all the rejection I had experienced almost all my life. I was also bitter that I was living in the body that I had created. Isa compared bitterness to someone who carries their pain with them, like a weighty load, that I literally was. Isa liked to talk in parables. He compared this bitterness as a person hauling animosity around with you was worse than dragging around a suitcase full of rocks. It is heavy and burdensome. The pain it inflicts on our heart is beyond description. If a person carries it on their back constantly, daily it gets heavier and heavier until you cannot stand it anymore. Then it starts to interfere with one's senses and actions. One will start to become illogical. You will start blaming everyone else for the things that go wrong, especially the ones you love dearest. Bitterness is a disturbing mental position and it triggers a wide range of other emotions, such as hating the people around you, even those who love you. One can become brutal, even self-harming, antagonistic and resentful, becoming anti-social, wanting to be alone. Isa also said being bitter leads to self-pity and vindictiveness and desires for revenge. A bitter person becomes his own worst enemy. It is very difficult to maintain any kind of relationship with a persistently bitter person and bitterness is a major contributing cause of marital and family problems.

This was the first time in my life I started to understand. I could see that my experiences in my childhood and teenage years had left a seed in me that had, over the years, grown bigger and bigger inside of me, taking over my body, emotionally and spiritually. This seed was called bitterness. Starting from the day the doctor diagnosed me as being too fat, to my school peers calling me those hurtful names, losing my first love, because of the rumour that I could not have children and me hating this body that I was born into, I had created the monster that I had become. Isa explained the bitterness within one's soul leads to consequential overtones. He continued to say, people who carried such heavy burdens would find it difficult to stay in a relationship without letting go. Isa was very intense in what he said. I wanted to be on my own to sit on a rock and reflect.

I had left my first wife, my children's mother as soon as someone else told me that they loved me, because I believed I deserved better. I then left the woman who pursued and loved me because I did not want to take responsibility of being a husband. I then spent the next ten years trying to convince this woman who once loved me to love me again. I was now so twisted that I had come to the conclusion that the only way out was that I wanted to kill myself. Whenever I drifted out and went into my own world Isa just carried on with what he was doing. This day things were different, as I sat balancing my thoughts and debating what next? Isa walked towards me with a smile on his face and something in his hand. At first, I thought it was a stone. It was a grey dirty oyster. He said, in a loud voice, "I'll bet everything I own that this has a pearl in it". I looked at him and thought that he did not own much, but got excited for him. Before I knew it Isa flicked the oyster open, splitting the shells apart. "I told you!" he shouted. "It's your Kismet," he said, passing the bottom part of the split shell to me. I refused to take it. I forgot about what I was thinking about in that minute and looked at this white thing, perfectly round and smooth lying stuck between one half of the oyster. "I have not seen one like this for years, it's yours, Isa shouted, at the same time forcing the shell into my hand. "No, it's not mine, you found it, it is yours, I am not going to take your find," I told Isa.

Then Isa started telling me about how a pearl was formed. He started to explain that a foreign body, such as a grain of sand, works its way into a particular species of oyster, mussel, or clam. As a defense mechanism, the oyster secretes a fluid to coat over the pain created by this foreign body. Layer upon layer of this coating is deposited onto the irritation until a radiant pearl is formed. As a result of this intrusion the oyster suffers injury and out of this suffering, a pearl is formed that can be worth a fortune. Isa then told me throughout life a person can experience a lot of suffering but this in a way can help to produce a person of great character within. In the course of all the difficult trials and pain that one has been through, regardless of the situation, remember that there is a plan for your life. This is the point in time for you to shine and not to appear dark and gloomy. Your home is a place you grow up waiting to leave and grow old wanting to go back to it, if you are not happy at home you will not be happy anywhere. He then said to me, "Go home son. Your best days are ahead of you, not behind you." He then stopped speaking, turned around and walked away.

I just looked at him and stood there on the rooks for about ten minutes, looking out at the sea. Isa was now repairing his net, looking for tears or big holes. It was then that moment just came to me, I did not want to die yet. I have unfinished business. I did not know at the time what this business was but all three mentors that I had met on the Bosphorus had made an impact on me, each one had taught me something about myself, they had enlightened me and woken me up. It was time to leave.

I walked back towards the hostel, towards Vedat's stall, expecting to find him selling simits. At first, I thought I had as usual lost my sense of any direction. I had sat on that stall enough times to know that Vedat had not set up the stall that morning. I asked the nearby newspaper seller if he had seen him. He looked at me as if he did not know me and I did not recognize him either. As I was talking to him, I somehow knew I was wasting my time. It was if I was speaking in a different language, he looked at me as if I was crazy so I just walked away. I waited a further few minutes but I could not see the stall anywhere. I thought I would come back later.

When I got to the hostel, Billy G was nowhere to be found either. I then started to get really alarmed, what was happening to me? I went into the reception area thinking I would find answers. It was deserted. I thought I would telephone the airline and see when I could fly out. I was lucky there was a flight to England the next day and decided I needed to be on that flight. So I arranged to leave the next day.

Packing a bag took minutes and I was ready to leave. I needed to say bye-bye to Isa and Vedat before I left. I woke up early, well, in truth I hardly slept. I went downstairs expecting Billy G to be at the reception. It was almost two days since his sister phoned him, he would never leave his business unattended. The cleaner, as usual, was mopping out the shower room that time in the morning. I asked her if he had seen Billy G and she looked at me puzzled and confused. I repeated my question. She now looked at me even more puzzled and shyly said something which I did not understand. I tried to make myself clearer but again felt I did not get through to her. I felt frustrated and very afraid. I could not leave without paying any money I owed, or even saying bye-bye. I could not trust anyone with any money, also I did not know what I owed. I needed to say bye-bye to Vedat and Isa and time was running out. I did not know what to do. I could not trust the Istanbul traffic so I thought I would ask a local taxi driver to take me to the airport, via going to see Vedat and Isa. I decided to write Billy G a note, giving him my phone number and address in London. I thanked him for looking after me and emphasized how much I had wanted to speak to him and say bye.

First stop was Vedat and as parking would be difficult in front of his stall, I told the driver to park near to the stall and I would run to Vedat say my bye-byes and be off. I told him I would not be more than five minutes. We drove towards the stall but I could not see it anywhere and did not know where Vedat was. I told the driver to drive further down the bank, hoping to find Vedat. No, I could not see him. I could feel the driver getting tense, as he was entering the morning rush. I tried to direct him but he told me that he could not go where I wanted him to go. He definitely would not be able to take me to the rocks, as the traffic would have led him onto the motorway towards the airport. I started getting upset, communication was breaking down. I told the driver to forget it. I fell back on my seat and thought that Vedat would be thinking where I had gone. Time was running out. My flight was three hours away and I could not trust the traffic. I needed to go.

Isa was my last stop. I was sure I would find him where he always is, he never wandered. Well, the taxi had no difficulty parking in front of the rocks but because of the time wasted looking for Billy G and Vedat, I needed to rush. I could not believe what was happening - Isa was nowhere to be found either! Everything looked so normal, just as I had known it for the past ten days or so. Isa's fishing equipment was present, his little mattress was there, and even signs of that morning's early catch were there. But there was no sign of Isa and no sign of Num Num. My first thought was Isa may be swimming so I looked out into the sea but I could not see him anywhere. Maybe he and the dog had gone to make a delivery. I waited for a few minutes, in case he was returning. I could see the taxi driver getting more impatient whilst waiting and I was so disappointed. I got into the car, sat down and thought that the situation was weird and surreal. In the past two weeks, I had met three people, my Bosphorus Disciples and they had all disappeared.

Returning back to a Life?

My journey to the airport was as lonely as when I had arrived. We made it to the airport with twenty-five minutes to spare. I made my way to the departure lounge. I looked in my wallet and still had some Turkish banknotes. I walked towards one of the bars that served alcohol and ordered a double Raki, poured some water into my glass and quickly drank it down. It tasted so nice, I sure had the taste for it. I ordered another double, drank that down too. Now my focus was to go back to England. The plane was quite empty and l could feel the Raki taking over, I was merry! I sat in the middle seat which was quite comfortable. There was no-one sitting by me on either side of me. No-one chose to sit next to me, we were all spoilt for choice. I looked out of the window, taking what I thought would be my last look at Istanbul.

Then from a distance, I could see the shape of three figures that looked very familiar. I stood up outside of my seat because I could not believe what I was seeing. I had to take a second look. The figures were three men and what looked like a small dog. A fat man was sitting down on something that looked like a stall in the middle of the other two, their body contours looking exactly like Billy G, Isa and Num Num. I felt a cold shudder running down my spine. To my amazement the three men started waving in a jubilant way at the plane. They looked very heavenly. I looked further, my mouth staying wide open. My astonishment was broken by a tap on my shoulder and one of the aircraft crew asked me to sit down as the plane was ready for take-off. I sat back into the seat, asking myself if I had imagined what I had just seen. Surely not. Was I drunker than I thought? Many questions were going about in my head. I could not believe what I had seen and the more I thought about it, I kept on saying to myself again and again "surely not". The three of them together, how did they get so close to the runway, with a dog too? I did not even know that they knew each other, I was very spooked by the whole affair and totally disturbed by what I had seen.

Well, it was all over. I could not do anything about it. I was now on the plane returning to the United Kingdom but at the time did not know what I was going back too. The only thing I was sure about was that I was on my way back. I had not planned that I would be doing this return journey. The 'fasten your seat belt' signs started flashing. I then tried to get the attention of one of the flight attendants. I needed an extension seatbelt and she obliged. Whilst walking towards me down the aisle I could see she had it in her hand. It was bright orange. All I could see were other passengers, sitting in their seats, turning back and looking towards me. All I could think have was them judging me and saying "look at that fat man, he needs an extension on his seatbelt". Whilst sitting back, reflecting and thinking about what I had experienced on the Bosphorus I decided it was time to do something about my weight. I would look into actually going on a diet. The flight back was as lonely as the one when I flew out. This time the four odd hours in the sky were consumed by me thinking of what I had experienced with Billy G, Vedat and Isa.

All three had played their parts in saving my life. Meeting the three Bosphorus disciples in Istanbul, was one of the greatest and profound moments in my life.

Landing back at Luton Airport and making my way through customs towards the bus terminal was long and never ending. It did not help that I was walking as slow as I could, just thinking. I asked myself what was the rush? I still slightly had doubts and felt that I had nothing to come back to. All I could think at the time was that I was returning to a single room in a house share. I did not even know if the room was there, I had not paid that months' rent, I relied on my initial deposit. At that moment I remembered another one of my father's famous stories about his father.

Apparently, my granddad, also called Naci, could not sleep one night. After tossing and turning for a few hours, he kept disturbing my grandmother who lay besides him and did not allow her to sleep. She asked my granddad what the problem was. He was a street food seller and business was very slow during that period. He continued to tell my Nan that he would not be able to pay the rent this month. My Nan, who was outwardly, a very loud plumpish short woman, was not afraid of anything. She got out of bed, pulled on her bloomers, wore her coat and in the middle of the night, walked about half a mile to the landlord's house. When she got there, she abruptly and as loud as she could, knocked on the landlord's front door. He quickly got out of his bed, stuck his head out of the upstairs window looking shocked and frightened. When he saw it was my Nan, he asked what was the matter, had the house burnt down? My Nan shouted as loud as she could, "No, we have not got the rent this month, so don't come to collect it." She then walked back to the family house, got into bed, looked at my granddad and instructed him to sleep, telling him "Now the landlord can't sleep!"

I loved that story. I now needed to kick myself out of this depression. I needed medical help, I could not do this on my own. One part of me was so scared. My previous choices, decisions, and ex-wives were clear indications of why I shouldn't be allowed to make decisions on my life. I had enough of being a slave to food. I needed to stop gambling full stop. Not an easy task. It was now time to reflect on my Bosphorus Disciples.

Vedat was and will always be my true role model. His life was the one that I really craved. In my eyes, he had everything that I would have wanted and he always remained humble. He seemed so content, he had a loving family, a job that he enjoyed and he controlled it rather than it controlling him. Everyone who knew him loved him. I envied the love that he shared with his wife. The only thing I regretted about meeting Vedat was that I could not tell him everything about myself because I could not even admit it to myself. I could not be honest to him, because of my shame, yet I'm sure he knew everything about me.

On the other hand, meeting up with Billy G was different. Sharing our short time together made me understand how bitterness and hatred can destroy a person. Most people have one love in their lives but do not end up with them. I had several and was with none of them. Billy G was surrounded by wealth but refused to benefit from it. He chose to hold himself back because of his past. He did not want to move on and live his life because of what had happened to him many years ago. The pain of not letting go had become twisted and physically crippled him. He hated the world but sadly hated himself more. Watching and listening to him taught me that every day we have plenty of chances to get angry, stressed or offended. However what you're doing when you indulge these negative emotions is giving something outside yourself power.

Isa was self-taught and wise. His major quality was his generosity, the fact that he would give you his last penny, his food and share all his wisdom with you. He chose to live his lifestyle outside of society's norms and had chosen to live his life the way he wanted to. Accepting the situation he found himself in, he had embraced what life had been given to him, not using any misfortune or disability as an excuse to not live life to the full. Maybe it was time that I picked a page from his book and I also did the same. I remembered what he once told me, "No one wants you when you have nothing, so what?" I now understood what he was trying to say. I always had trouble understanding why the people in the past that I had helped, in one way or another hated me so much. Now I was asking myself, "yeah, so what?" Isa was very wise and spiritually was very inspiring; he was very philosophical and taught me about my inner self and how to break loose from the chains that were holding me down. Sometimes he gave me answers without even saying anything. He, most importantly I felt, made me think differently about how I should see life and how I should interpret it.

I now had the same life but looked at it completely in a different way. My understanding, my attitude had changed, those old clichés returned such as "life was to short", or that "you are a long time dead". Now life was full of smiles and I felt that I had been released. I no longer lived in fear of being alone, or of what I would with my time. I was not dependent or addicted to outsiders or the factors of society. I would no longer thrive on rejection or rely on someone to love me.

I no longer needed to escape or hide from anything. What was supposed to be the end had now become my beginning.

Musings

I really do hope that I may have helped someone who can identify with my book. Mental illness is a complex issue. Addiction is fairly wide-ranging.

The Merriam-Webster Dictionary defines addiction 'as a compulsive need for and use of a habit-forming substance characterized by tolerance and well-defined physiological symptoms upon withdrawal; persistent compulsive use of a substance known by the user to be harmful'.

Simply, addiction is the loss of control over your life as a result of your abuse of a substance or an activity.

Truthfully, most people suffer from some form of addiction during their lifetime, whether or not they realize it and seek recovery. Until I started to write my book I never realized just how many addictions I had. My eating disorder is now more recognized as a mental disorder. Simply put, I have an abnormal eating habit that negatively affects my physical or mental health. I suffer from a binge eating disorder where I eat a large amount in a short period of time.

"Some people who are obsessed with food become gourmet chefs. Others become eating disorders." — Marya Hornbacher, Wasted: A Memoir of Anorexia and Bulimia

I would often talk with others about my life experiences, most of the time putting some sort of humour into my stories, or just talking about the funny things that ever happened in my past. Planning and writing this book has been a significant journey in my life. At times, I felt I needed to put my life on show. My ultimate aim was to write and if possible get it published, however unlikely. To publish a book to give to everyone who ever listened and enjoyed the segments of my life and they suggested that I should write this book. I also wanted to leave some sort of legacy for my children. If either one has the patience and strength to get to know me, try to get some answers to some questions they may want to ask, why I did what I did? How this came about? Mostly though, I decided to write this book for me, to tell my story to myself. I needed to understand me, what made me.

I tried to touch on everything that I could remember, writing down things as I remembered them. Being honest was the easiest part, writing the personal parts were a lot harder, I have also tried to avoid, as much as I can, the negatives of others, firstly because they have not got a chance to answer back. I also do not have any desire to appear in any more court cases. The arrogant side of me knows what I know. Writing the first draft was very difficult, very painful and it hurt. It hurt so much that in a matter of a few seconds I took the rational decision to delete every word I had patiently written over eighteen months and cleared any trace of it on my PC.

My inner soul, that voice in my head, would keep asking me why I had stopped, when was I going to restart? When I did start rewriting I kept stopping and starting. Why I was not writing at that moment? When are you going to write, some more? You need to finish it. You need to find closure. Hating one's self and carrying the weight of bitterness, anger or eventually contemplating suicide.

Writing became an obsession. It was a big part in my life, but before I started I did not in any way envisage how much time and energy I would have devoted to it. I think I have never before put so much vigorous devotion to anything I had started before. I had started many things but rarely finished them. Writing this book has at times been very torturous and life-destroying. Maybe I forcefully carried on as an extension of my self-harming, going back in life and thinking about what happened, why it happened and how I dealt with it. It was as if I had lifted old paving slabs to find all sorts of creatures and monsters working underneath. The challenge was resurrecting these issues that I thought were closed and I had moved on from, writing about them and afterward being able to file them away again. Reviving all these old memories would stay in my head, for days, even weeks. When I slept, I dreamed about whatever scenario I wrote about during that day and come up with an alternative solution. Temptations and desires were consistently coming into play, urges to telephone people, just to ask how they are were, depressingly haunting me. Writing the book made me moody and sometimes touchy and delicate. I would often take time off sometimes, months at a time even years, refusing to look at it, at times I even started to hate this book.

Well, I have finally written this book. 'The book' is really finished (or is it?). I cannot add to it anymore. At this moment I suppose I can start to write the sequel but what would I talk about? This book has been my achievement. I did it. A Turkish Cypriot man who struggled to get a qualification in the English language, a person who has never, ever read another book, from the beginning to the end. It has taken me over ten years to tell my story.

Acknowledgements

I thank many people who know who they are, who have listened to me saying words like 'the book', 'my book', 'it's in the book' or 'read my book' again and again for over a decade. I thank those who have draft read it, bored them, hurt them but they still read it. If it was not for them I would have stopped, these people kept the book alive, they gave the book its spirit. I thank those who deep down were fed up of me telling them about the book, those who did not even believe that the book really existed. Thank you to the Lammer's Legends Who I bored to death talking about me and writing a book. Thank you to Lynda Humphry my secret, virtual friend who got me through my Bell's Palsy, in Turkey and seemed to know whenever I was down or going down and was there to cheer me up many times.

My biggest thank you is to Ian Bailey who never gave up on me, nagged me to start writing and rewriting. He never stopped from the first word that I put on paper. Secondly, thanks to Pamela McFarlane who made me so jealous when she showed me her completed book? *'The Lucky Bean Tree'* I showed her my attempt and her words were the inspiration I needed to carry on and finish. But lastly I must thank all those in my book for being part of my life, they were the biggest part. However if you were not mentioned you still played a part. I finally would like to thank those who never knew me, but know me now, as they are now reading my book. I need to also apologize to humbly thank V.A.N who was the first person to read my rough second attempt and patiently and gently nagged me to finish 'the book' for over five years, encouraging me to start writing again and again, but I could not find the oomph to restart writing again, until now. Thank you so much V.A.N.

Lisa's Story

For years I was the fat girl with the blonde hair and big thighs,
People would tell me "oh but you could be so pretty as they
inwardly sighed,

Never had a thigh gap, could not bend to tie my shoes and my
belly wobbled as I walked,
I would look to the ground, cry and pretend to not hear the
nasty comments of strangers as they talked,

Who ate all the pies, are you pregnant, you're such a fat girl, 3
chinned Lisa, I have heard it all,
And for so many years I would feel defeated, grab that extra
cake and curl up at night exhausted by it all

For years I pasted on a smile, laughed at myself with others
and cried myself to sleep,
Never letting on that those comments, however well-meant
would cut me so very deep,

Walking up hills was a battle and I'd feel like I was having a
cardio arrest,
Pains in my spine, my knees and chronic asthma but I still tried
my best,

I learned from a young age that I could never be what others
wanted and not just because of my size,
So I hit back with sarcasm, would cover myself up with
oversized clothing and inwardly I cried,

Now I am physically smaller and can fit comfortably into an
armed seat,

I can walk up a hill without pause and when I bend I can reach
my feet,

But when I look in the mirror I don't see a 9 stone weight loss
and get embarrassed when people comment at my new shape,
I still see the fat girl with the big thighs, double chin and hear
those nasty comments as if they are on tape,

Finally I have realised that I am me, with curves, wobbly bits
and lots of imperfections,
But my imperfections make me, and I have finally accepted
that without exception,

This journey has taught me many things and I have learned to
love myself for me and for the first time I have a shape that I
want to keep,
But the biggest lesson has been that I am OK the way I am, fat,
thin, tall, short, and that beauty really is only skin deep.

Written by Lisa Abbott.

"Empty Space" James Arthur

I don't see you
You're not in every window I look through
And I don't miss you
You're not in every single thing I do
I don't think we're meant to be
And you are not the missing piece

I won't hear it
Whenever anybody says your name
And I won't feel it
Even when I'm burstin' into flames
I don't regret the day I left
I don't believe that I was blessed
I'm probably lyin' to myself again

I'm alone in my head
Looking for love in a stranger's bed
But I don't think I'll find it
'Cause only you could fill this empty space
I wanna tell all my friends
But I don't think they would understand
It's somethin' I've decided
'Cause only you could fill this empty space

Space, space
This empty space
Space, space
This
'Cause only you could fill this empty space

I've been drinking
I've been doin' things I shouldn't do
Overthinking
I don't know who I am without you
I'm a liar and a cheat
I let my ego swallow me
And that's why I might never see you again

I'm alone in my head
Looking for love in a stranger's bed
But I don't think I'll find it
'Cause only you could fill this empty space
I wanna tell all my friends
But I don't think they would understand
It's somethin' I've decided
'Cause only you could fill this empty space

Space, space
This empty space
Space, space
This
'Cause only you could fill this empty space

DAD

07-07-37 - 23-9-16

REST IN PEACE IN PARADISE

Sorry Dad, you know I was never good at finishing what I ever started. Well I have finally completed my book. Unfortunately you couldn't wait. I'm sure though you know I have finished it. Thank you; for being my dad: Mr. Vedat..

MISSING YOU

L - #0109 - 020919 - C0 - 210/148/12 - PB - DID2607569